Mushroom Magic

A Magical Design Coloring Book

48 Designs for You to Color & Enjoy

By Katie Darden & Billy Bush

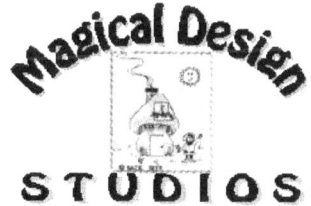

Magical Design STUDIOS

www.MagicalDesignStudios.com

ISBN: 1541022513
ISBN-13: 978 -1541022515

Books in the *Digital Mandala* Series
~*~
Full Sized (8x10) or Pocket Sized (5.25x8)

Heart~2~Heart
Star Gazing
FloraBunda
Round & Round
Square Roots

Books in the *All You Need Is LOVE* Series
~*~
Full Sized (8.5x11) - Pocket Sized (5.25x8)coming soon

All You Need is LOVE
All You Need is LOVE 2
LOVE is All You Need (coming soon)

Books in the *WORDS* Series
~*~
Full Sized (8.5x11) - Pocket Sized (5.25x8)coming soon

Words to LIVE By
Words to LOVE By (coming soon)
Just Say NO to Sweary Words

Santa Season Sampler Series
~*~
Full Sized (8.5 x11) or
As card sets

Volume 1 - Santa and His Elves
Volume 2 - Christmas Cheer
Volume 3 - Candlelight
Volume 4 - Stuffed Stockings

And the Full Set - Volumes 1-4
with bonus images

Some books also available in comb-bound versions, pdf versions and card sets at our Etsy Store:
http://Etsy.com/shop/MagicalDesign

INTRODUCTION FROM KATIE

The fantasy mushrooms in this book were hand drawn by me and my grandson, Billy Bush. I've long appreciated mushrooms – even the Magical Design Studios logo (designed in 1977) features an elf in a mushroom house. It turns out that Billy has become an amateur mycologist, and between the two of us, we designed this book for your enjoyment and ours.

Some of the drawings and designs are exclusively mine. Others are exclusively Billy's. But most are a combination of the two of us, where Billy might draw the overall shape, and I would fill in details. Along with the mushrooms, we've included several mandalas digitally created using the mushroom drawings. I can promise you, you are not likely to find these mushrooms anywhere except in your and our imagination.

Billy would often visit us for several weeks at a time when he was younger, and he and I often worked on projects together that involved hand-dying of fabrics and tshirts, making glass jewelry and windchimes, wire-wrapping stones and glass, machine sewing pillows and crafts, and various forms of painting. At least, we'd do these things when I could 'pry' him away from the rocket-scientist projects he and his Papa Tom were involved in. Just like his mom, his artistic style and eye is different from my own, and that's part of what made this project such fun for me.

The 'art' of coloring has become the latest endeavor for helping us as we seek peace and calmness from our crazy world. The process of coloring can actually become a form of meditation. And meditation is simply inward focus. What comes from that experience is individually yours. Mandalas are a spiritual and ritualistic symbol in both Hinduism and Buddhism, that generally represents the Universe. The word "Mandala" comes from Sanskrit. According to Wikipedia, the basic form of most mandalas is a square with four gates containing a circle with a center point. Each gate is in the general shape of a T.

Over the years, and especially after its introduction to the west, "mandala" has become a generic term for diagrams or geometric patterns that represent the cosmos metaphysically or symbolically. In other words, they represent a microcosm of the universe. When most of us think of mandalas, we picture repeating patterns within a circular format, like slices of a pie. In this book, they are mushroom pies.

The mandala is used to help focus attention on spiritual guidance, and for mindful practices such as meditation. The circle has long been a spiritual symbol of wholeness. It's used in astrology, religion, and many kinds of spiritual rituals and traditions. The Native American Medicine Wheel and Dreamcatcher are two examples of the circle as a spiritual focus of wholeness.

But the use of mandalas isn't just spiritual. Therapists as far back as Carl Jung have used mandalas with their patients. Through his own experiences, Jung recognized that the urge to make mandalas emerged during moments of intense personal growth. He discovered, according to Wikipedia, "Their appearance indicates a profound re-balancing process is underway in the psyche. The result of the process is a more complex and better integrated personality."

As a business and career coach, my partner and I used a process that incorporated our Balance Wheel, a mandala-like approach that helped people develop a balanced career, business, and life focus.

As an artist and an adult, I've been designing mandalas for over 40 years, incorporating them into my watercolor and silk paintings, as well as my fabric dying and the quilts I design and construct. I even sell reproductions of these as cards at crafts fairs and in my Etsy store. I find mandalas are nearly as therapeutic to create as they are to color. The choices of colors and arrangements are so vast that no two people will ever end up with mandalas that look the same, even if they're using the same exact design.

In this book you will find a variety of designs, with various levels of complexity, and in no particular order. We hope you enjoy using the patterns in this book as much as we did in creating them.

At the very end of this book you will find a Color Chart you can use to test out your pens, pencils, markers, chalk, paints, etc. to see how they look on this paper. Remember every paper is different, and your tools will look different on each of them also. Feel free to copy the sheet first so you can use it if you decide to color on photocopy images.

HOW TO USE THIS BOOK

Katie is a lifelong artist and crafter. As a painter and illustrator, she generally prefers to do her design work and illustrations by hand. But she also trained in computer animation in the mid-80s and she does love what computers can do. Many of her coloring books include both hand-drawn and electronically-drawn illustrations for you to enjoy, as well as hand-drawn illustrations that have been digitally manipulated (such as the mandalas in this book).

There are several ways you can use the drawings in this book. You may choose to color or draw directly on the pages, but you can also photocopy them first so you can use the images more than once. Do whatever makes sense to you.

Most people will simply color the drawings to bring them to life. However, feel free to use other illustration techniques, such as crosshatching or using patterns or symbols such as circles or bubbles, to fill in the spaces - in color or black and white. Also feel free to augment the drawings if you want. These are now your pictures to do with as you wish for your personal purposes. The only restrictions is that you can't sell or use the designs in any commercial endeavor. I'm sure you understand, these are our original illustrations.

Once you begin to work with colors, there are several different approaches you can take. Anything that will mark on or create color on paper can be used - crayons, colored pencils, marking pens, chalk, pigments, watercolor or acrylic paints, or even glitter glue. You can even mix your media if you want, or use more than one color to shade or shadow the designs. If you decide to use paints or highly liquid media, you will want to tape your paper to something flat to help prevent buckling, removing the tape once dry, as they do with watercolor paintings.

When thinking about your design, you may want to consider basic color theory in choosing your palette. While we could spend several pages explaining basic theory to you, in today's world, there are several online resources that can do a better job. We recommend you search on Google, Yahoo or Bing. We found two sites that were especially helpful: ***http://www.colormatters.com/color-and-design/basic-color-theory***, which includes the basics and ***http://www.tigercolor.com/color-lab/color-theory/color-theory-intro.htm#Color_Wheel*** which explains how to select harmonious colors for your masterpiece. In regards to colors, pay attention to what is discussed regarding *analogous* colors (those next to each other on the wheel), *complementary* colors (those opposite each other), and color *context/contrast*. Also consider the issues of *tint* (colors mixed with white) and *shade* (colors mixed with black) - also referred to as *value* - and the issue of *saturation* (how intense or dull the color is).

You'll find two color wheels on the back cover. The one with the triangles in the middle is the most basic of wheels. The inner triangle points to the *primary* colors (red, yellow, blue). The colors in the outer triangle are the *secondary* colors (orange, green, purple). The *tertiary* colors are those between the primary and secondary colors. The color wheel with several concentric circles shows **values** (lightest in the center, to darkest on the outside). Experiment. Then use what you've discovered to plan your color scheme.

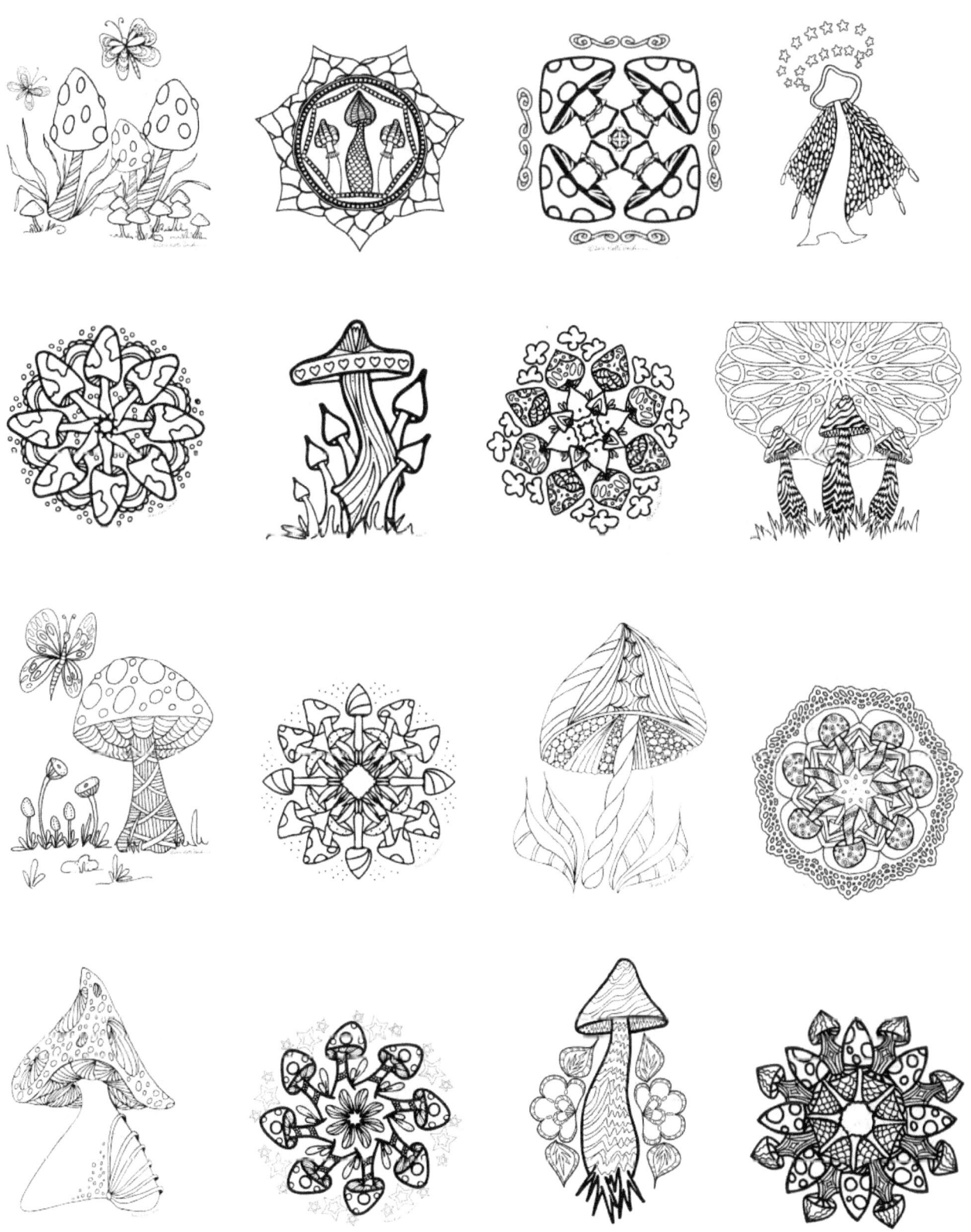

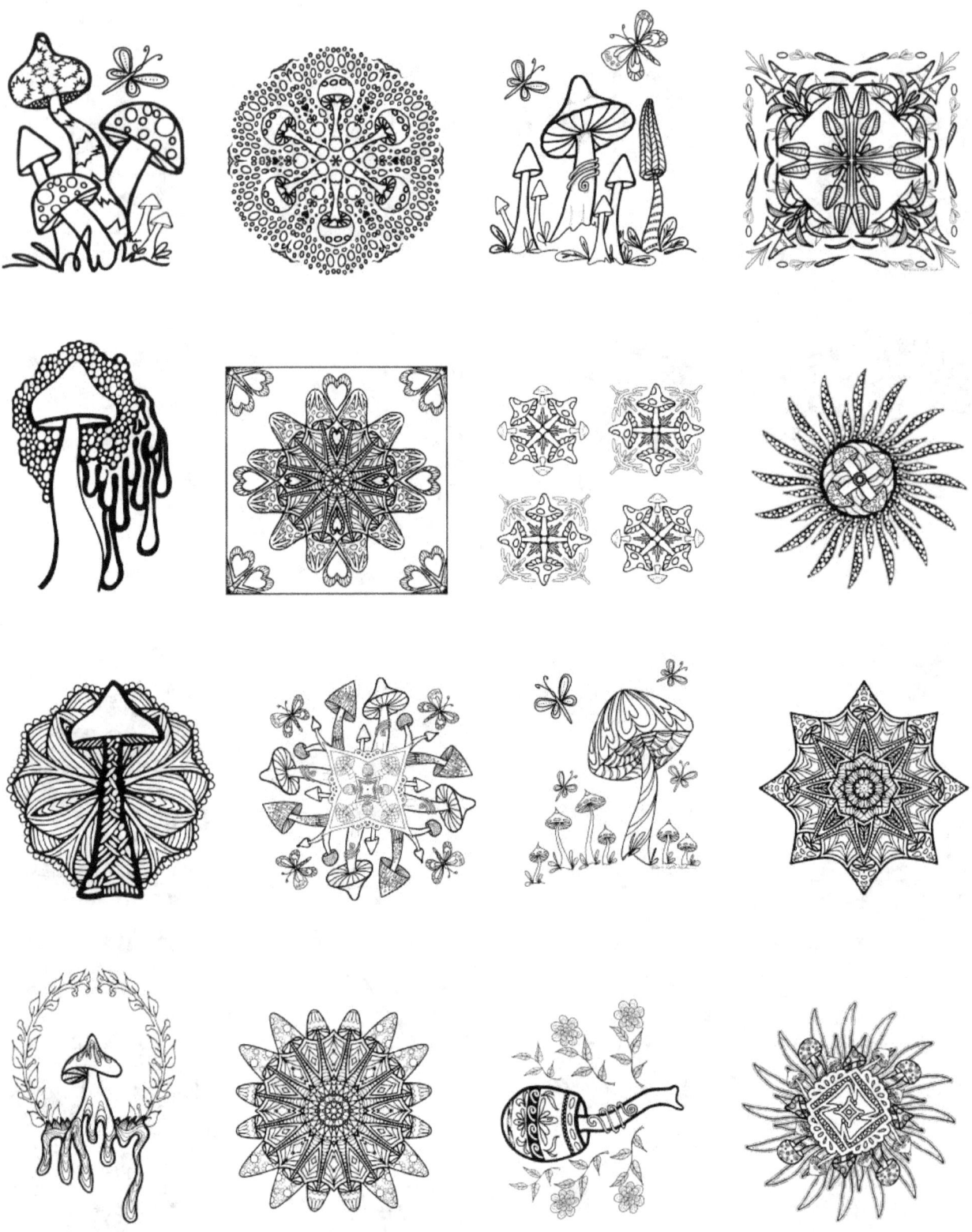

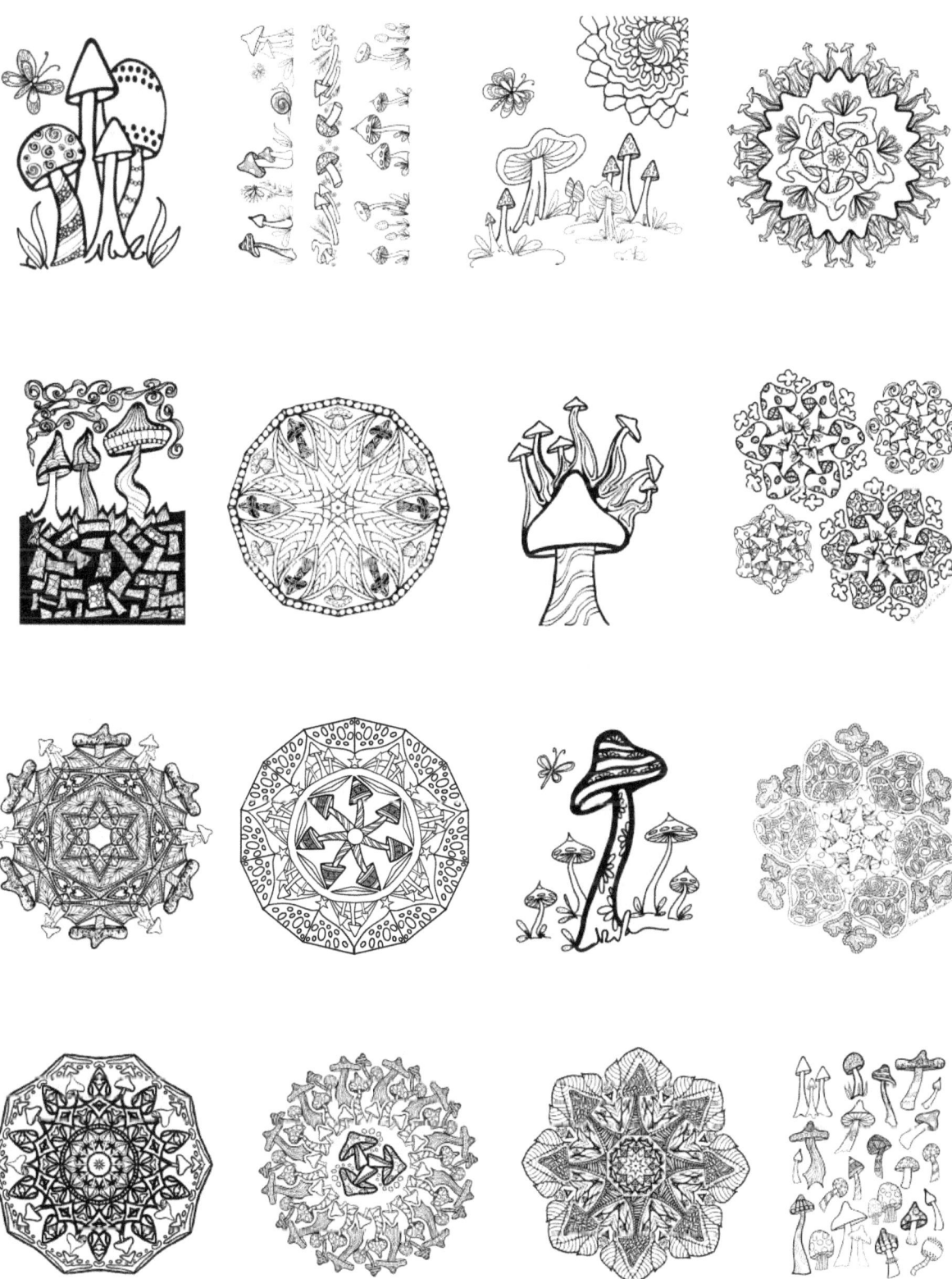

Mushroom Magic

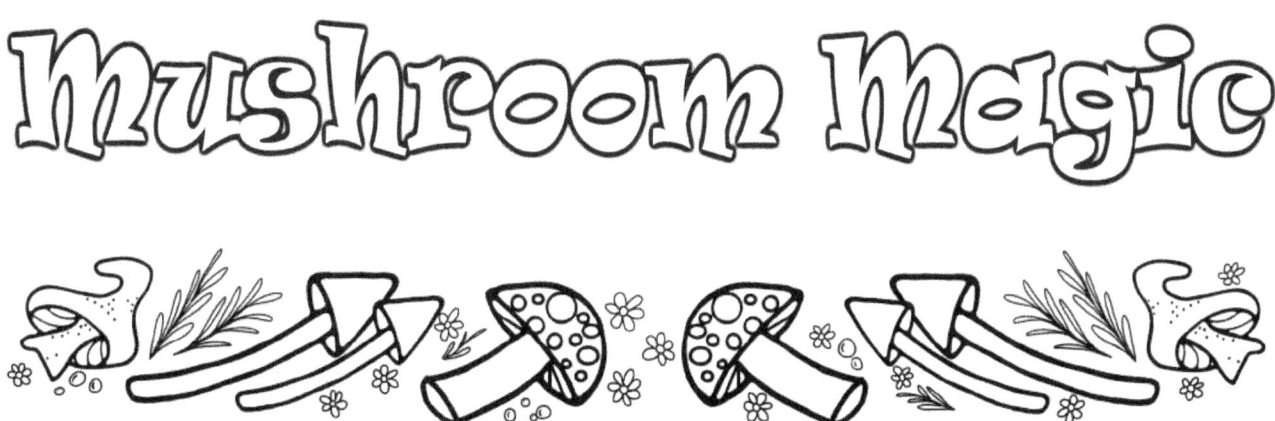

48 Designs for You to Color & Enjoy

NOTE:

Pens or liquid coloring used on these pages may bleed through to the page below. Be sure to use paper or thin cardboard between the pages if you chose to color directly in this book rather than to color on a photocopy.

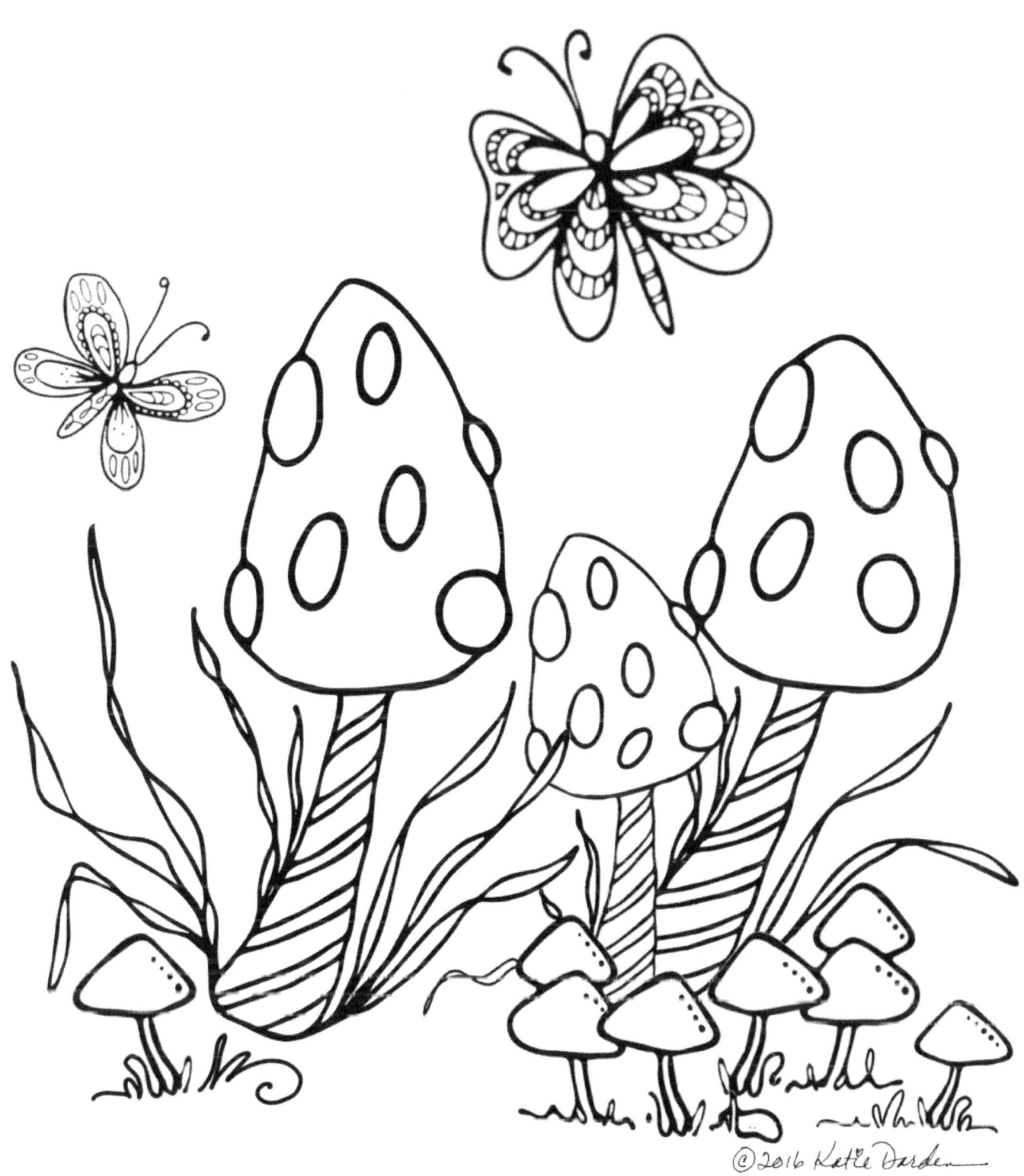

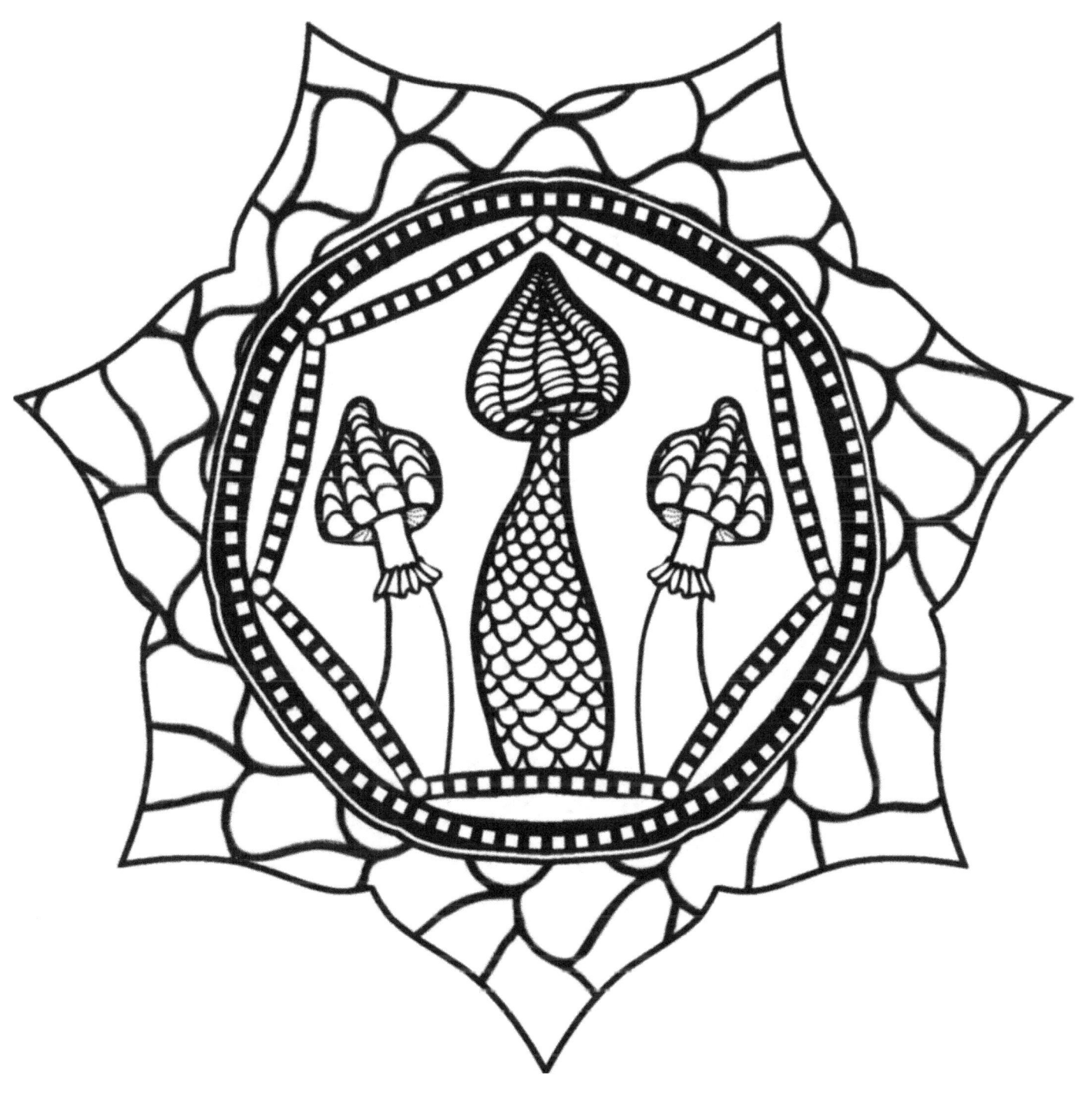

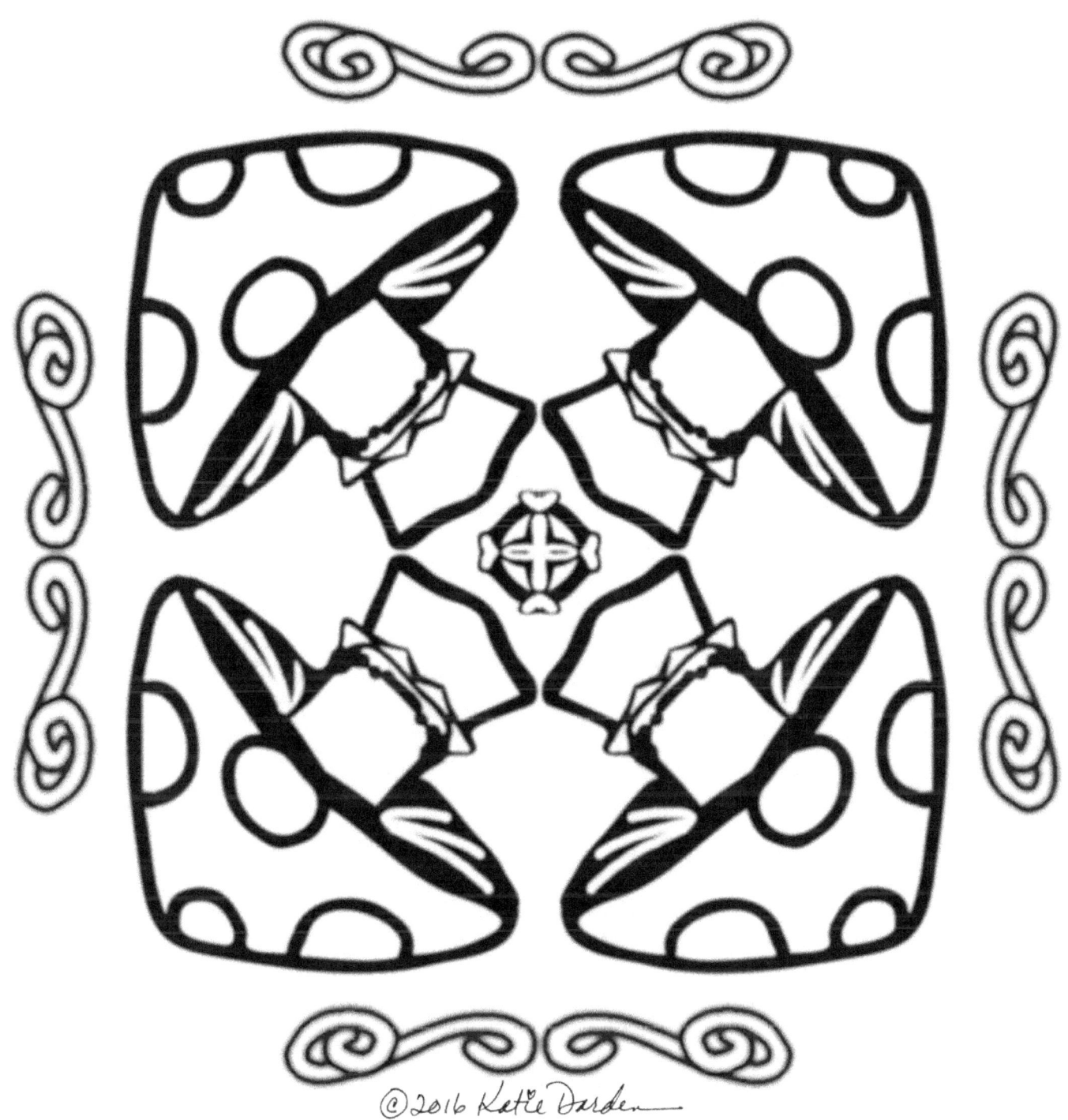

©2016 Katie Darden

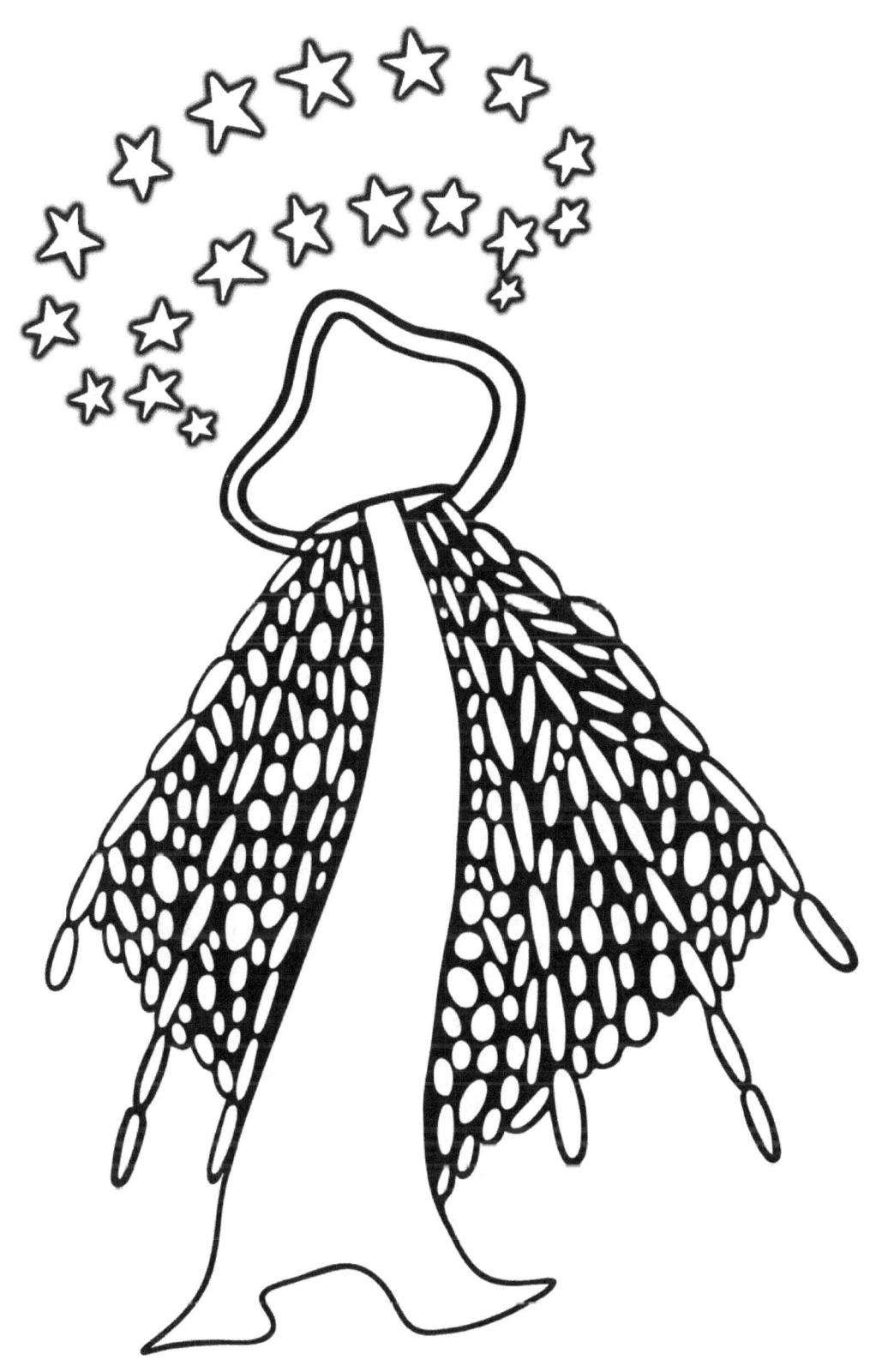

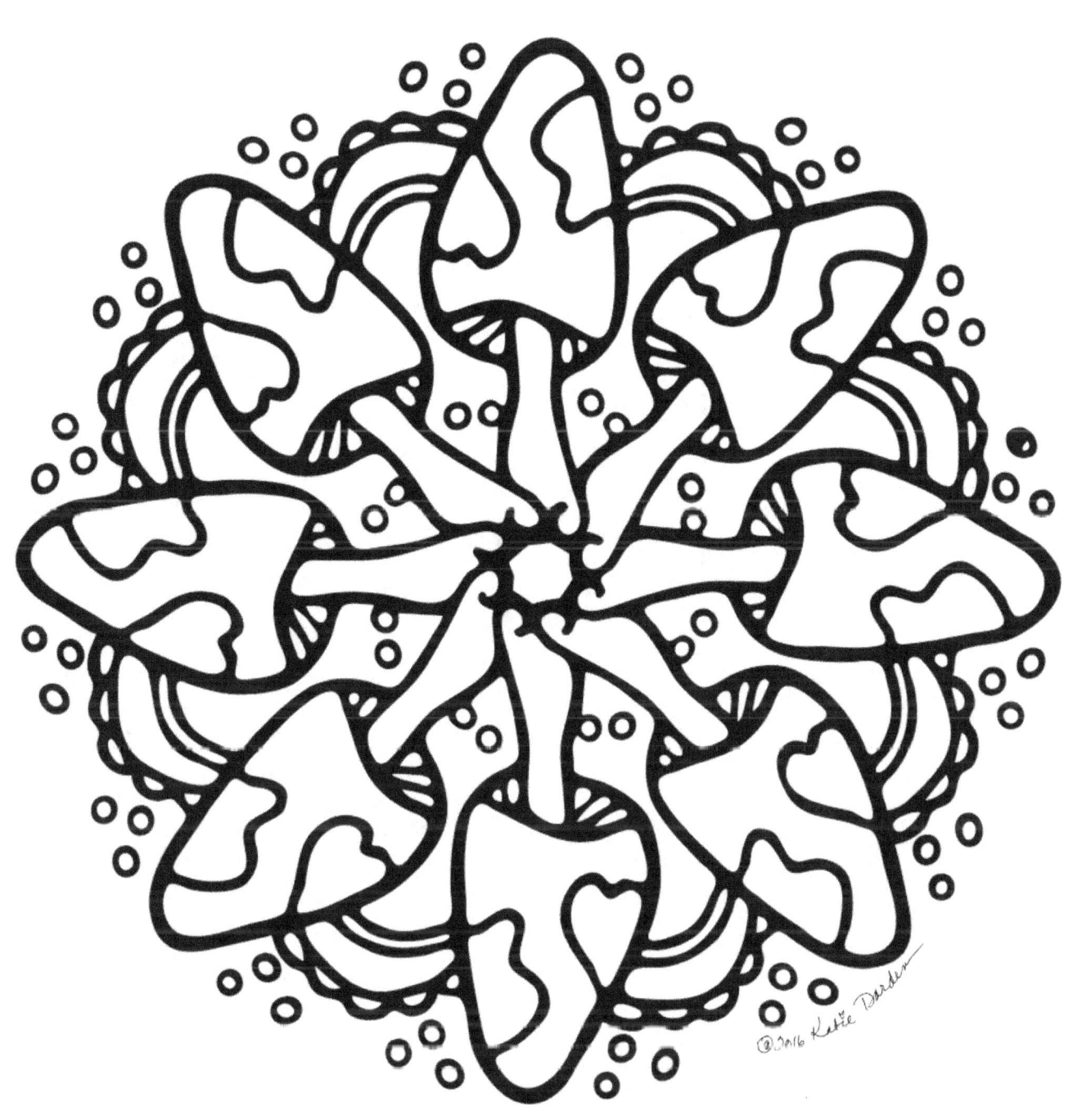

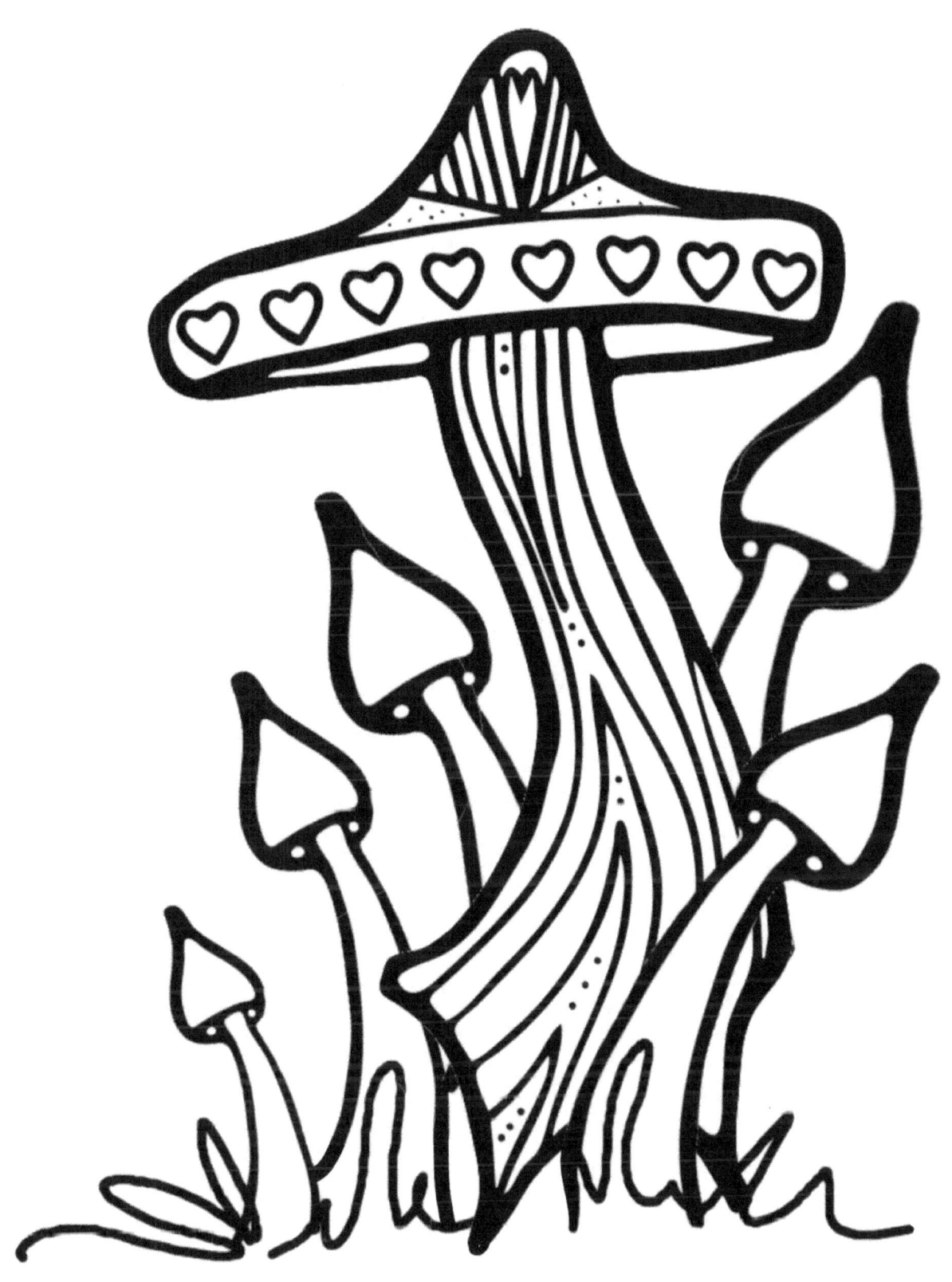

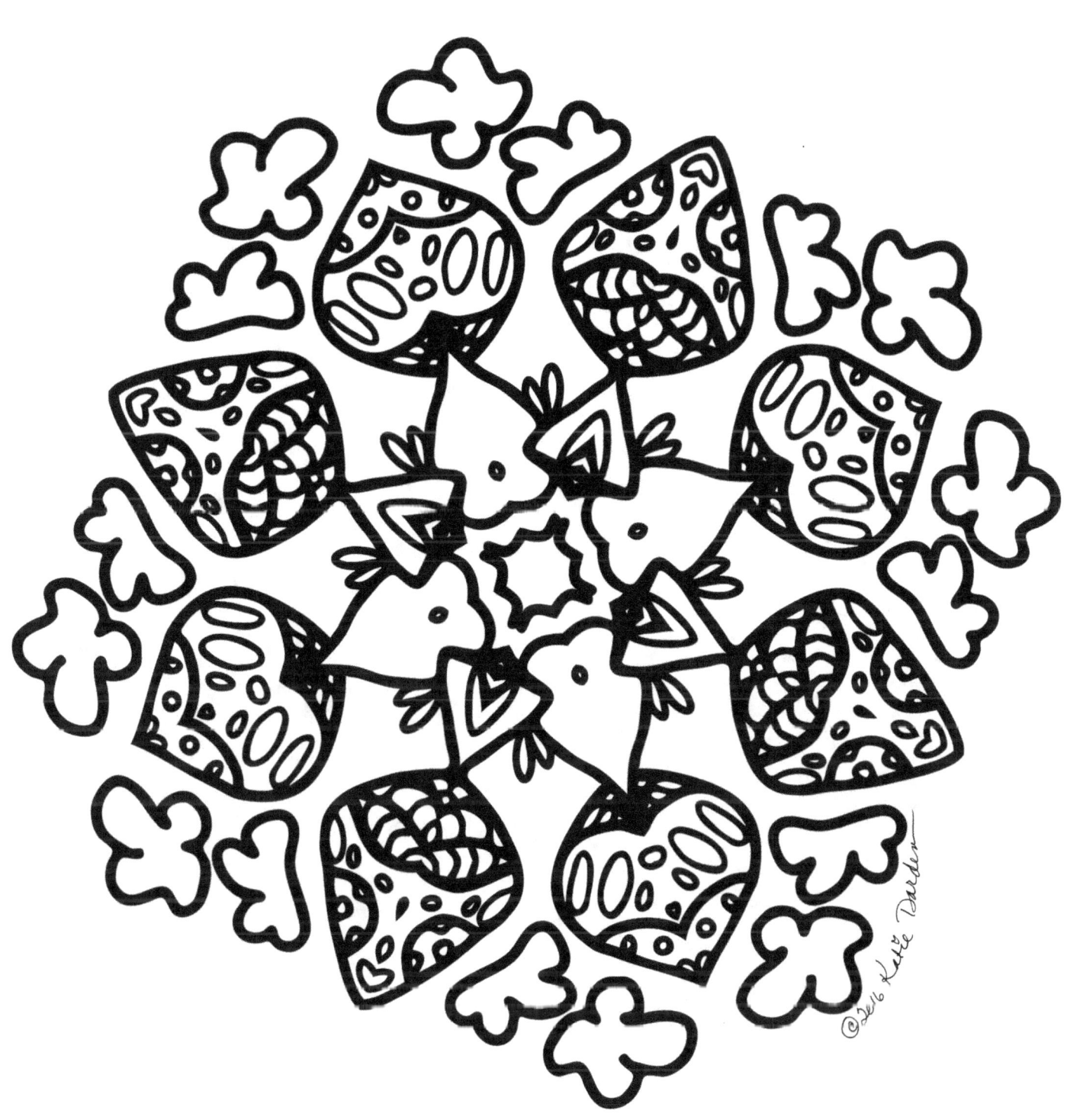

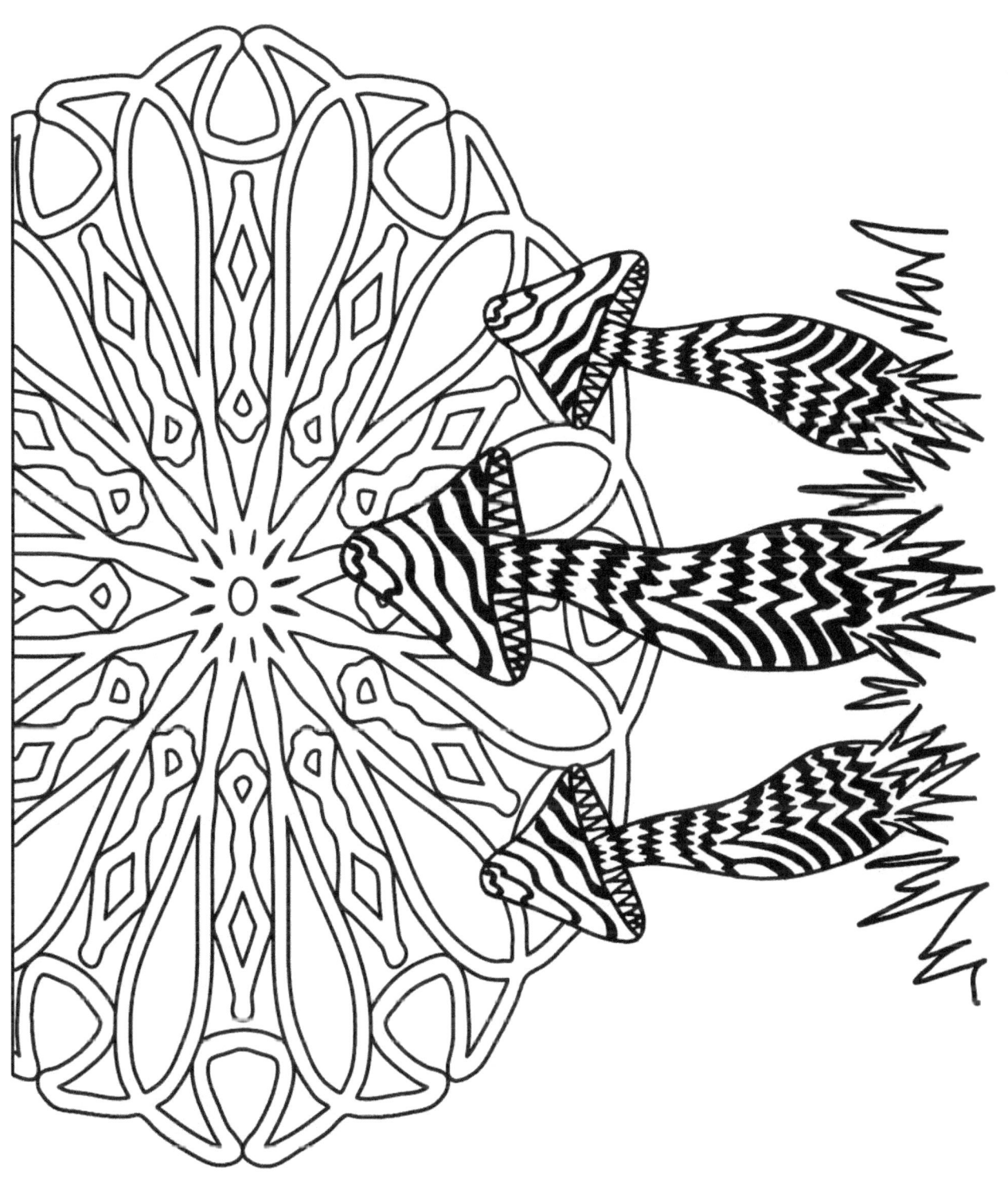

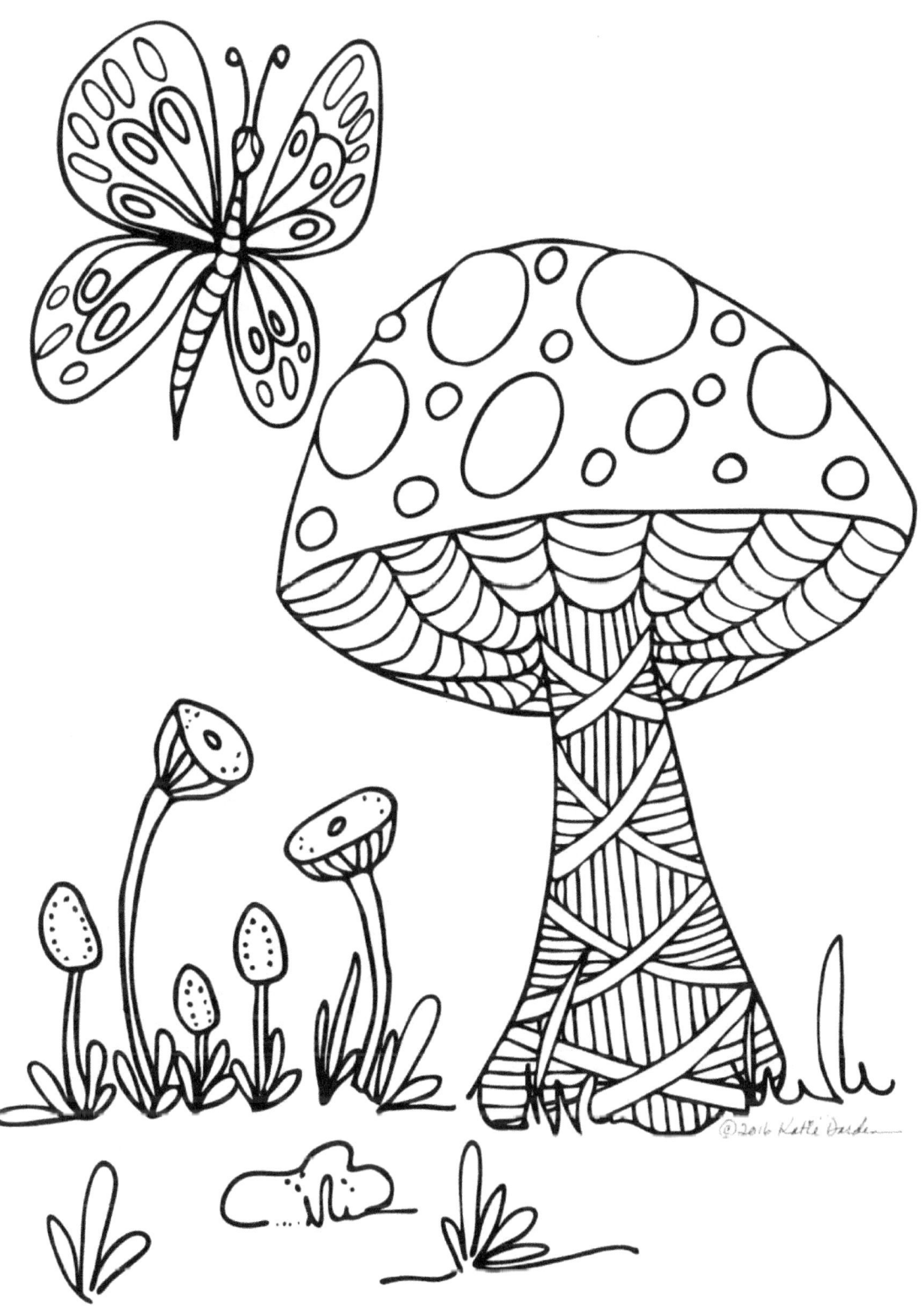

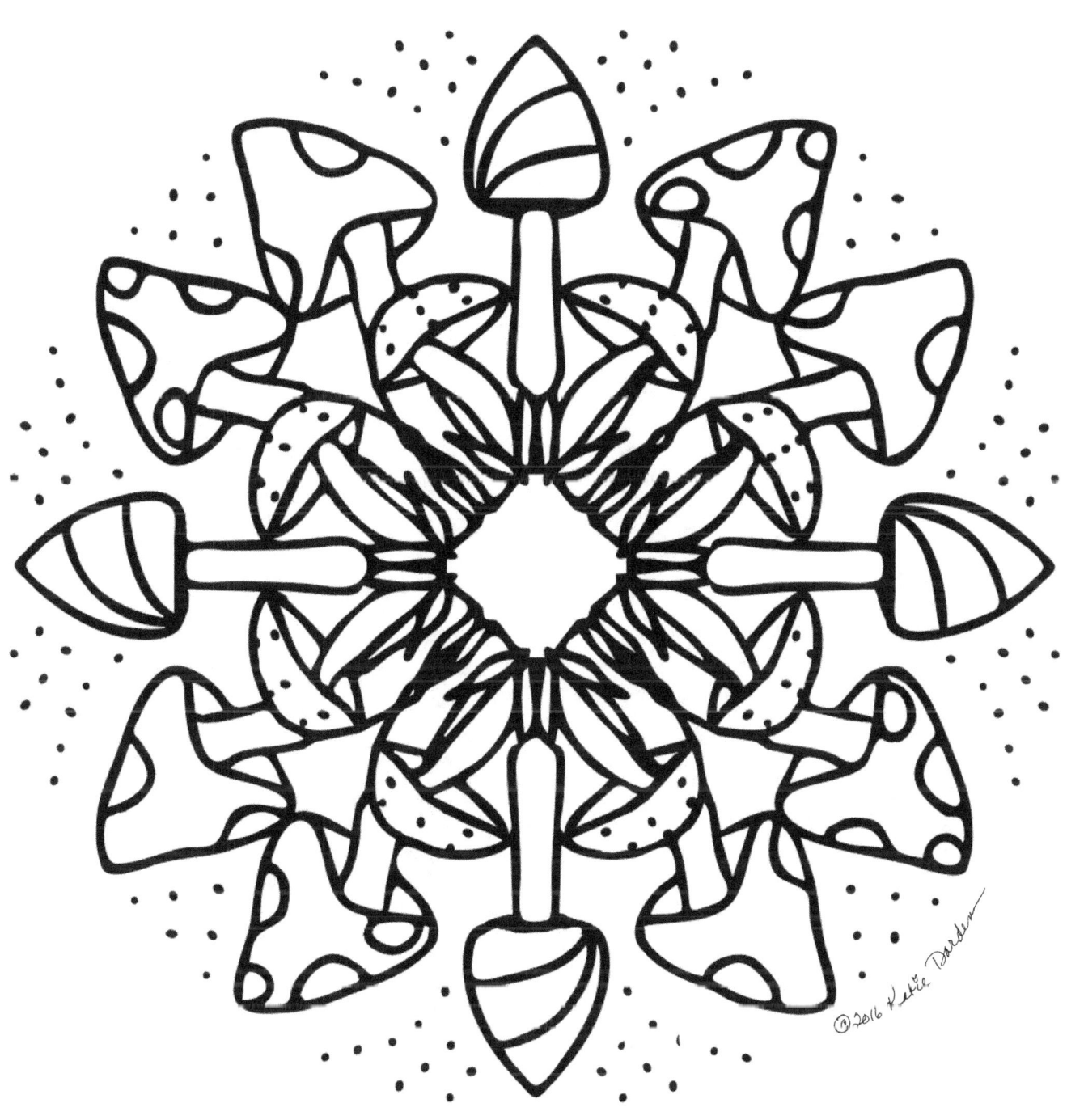

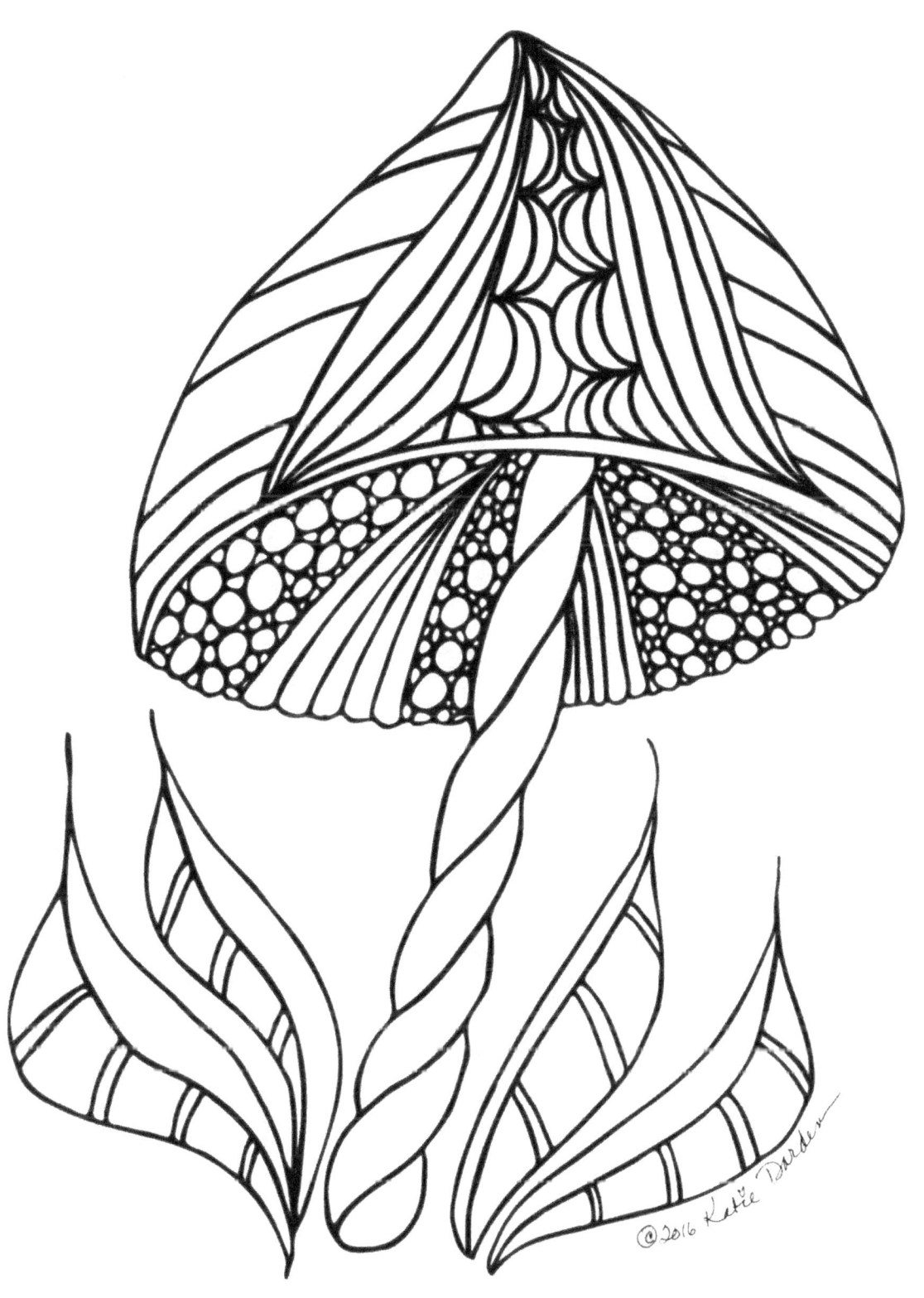

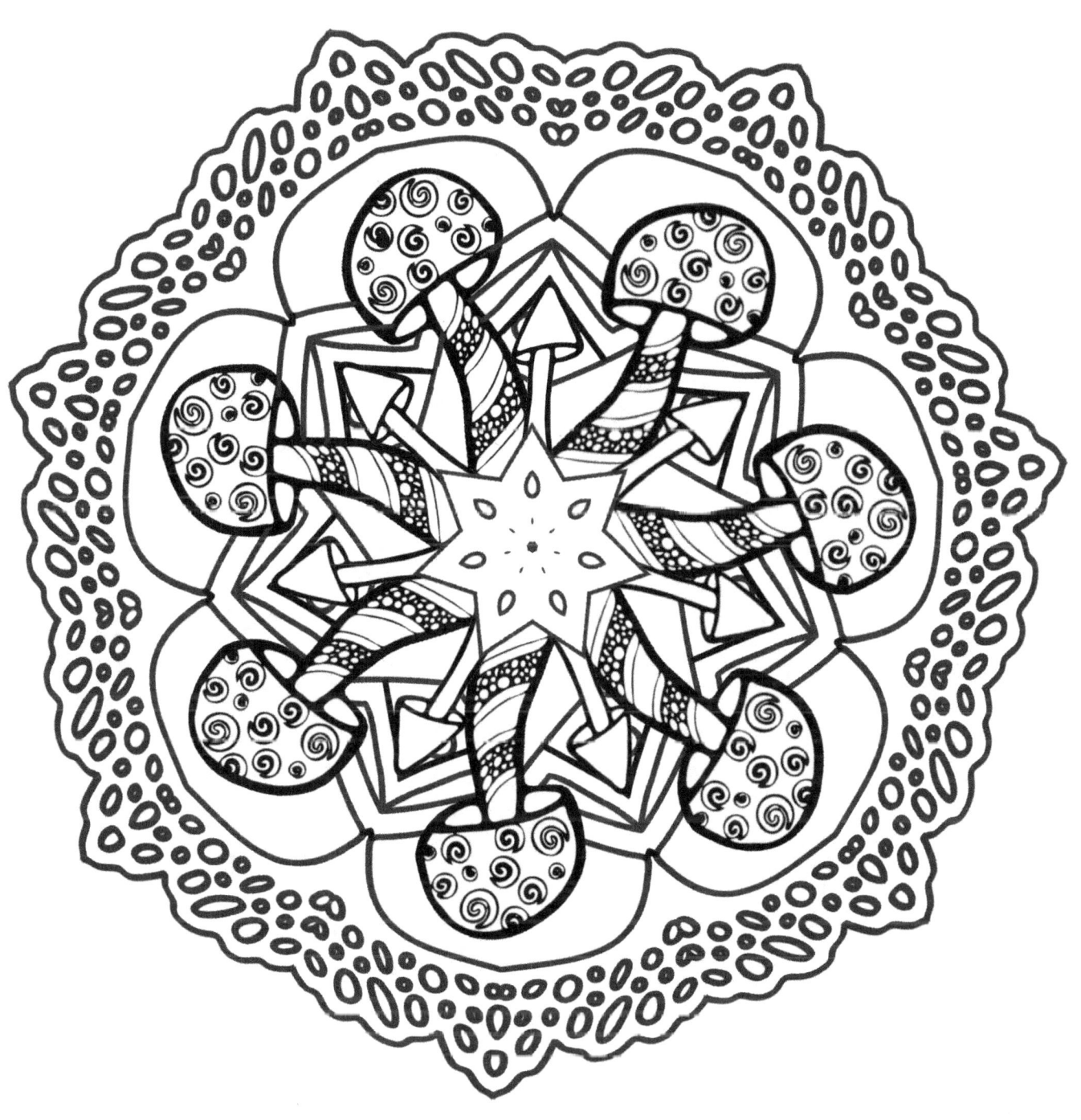

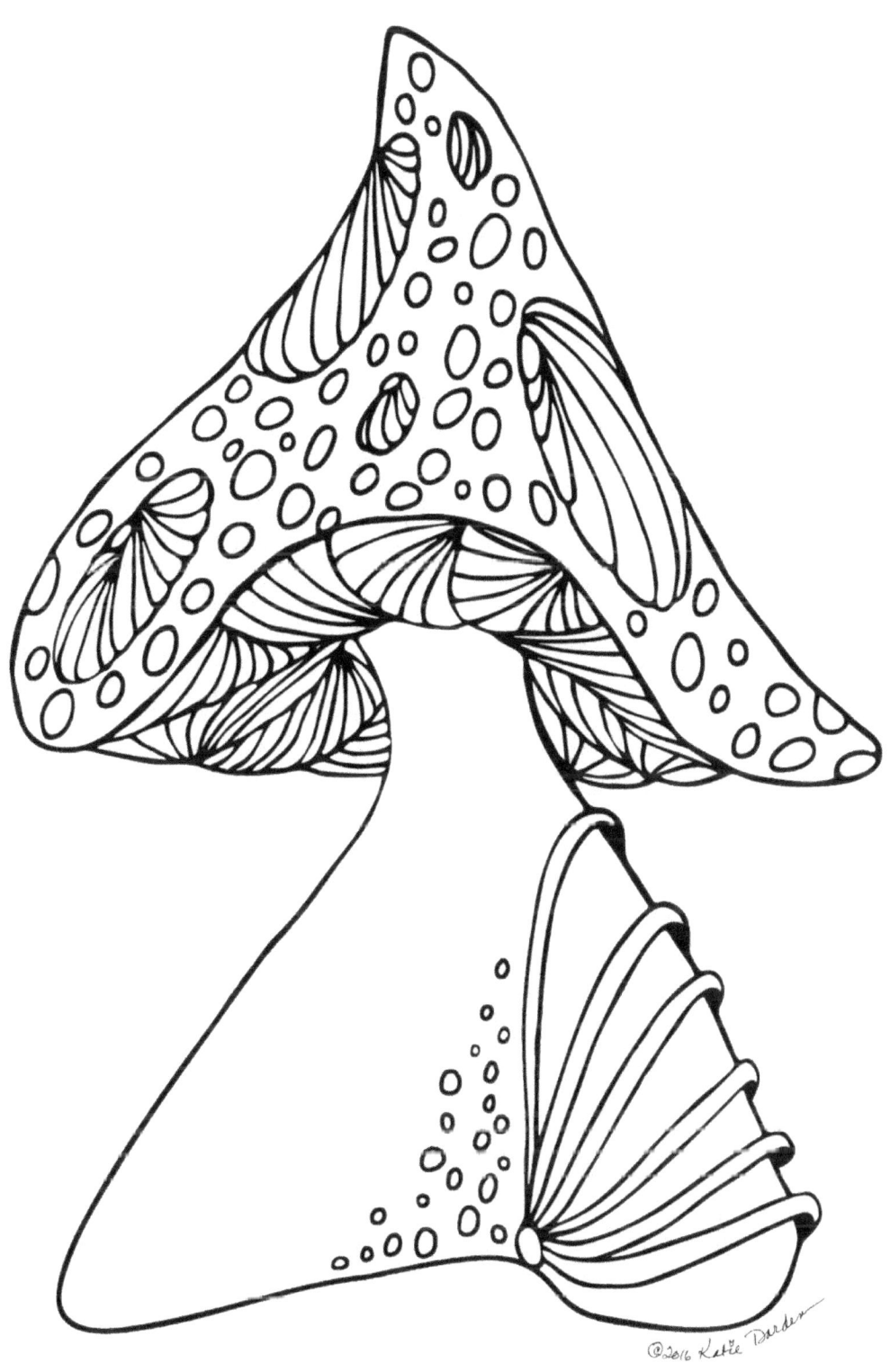

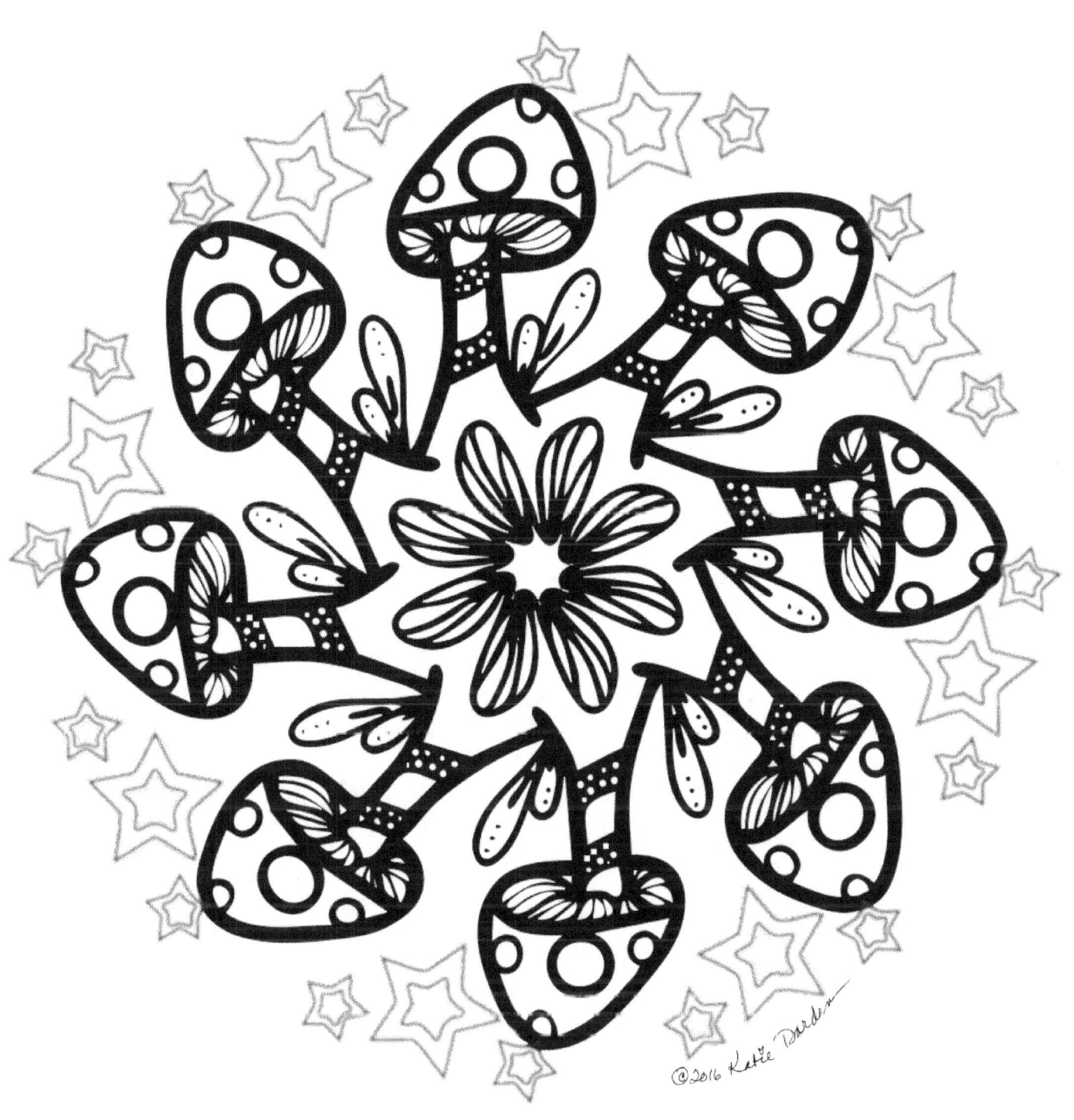

©2016 Katie Darden

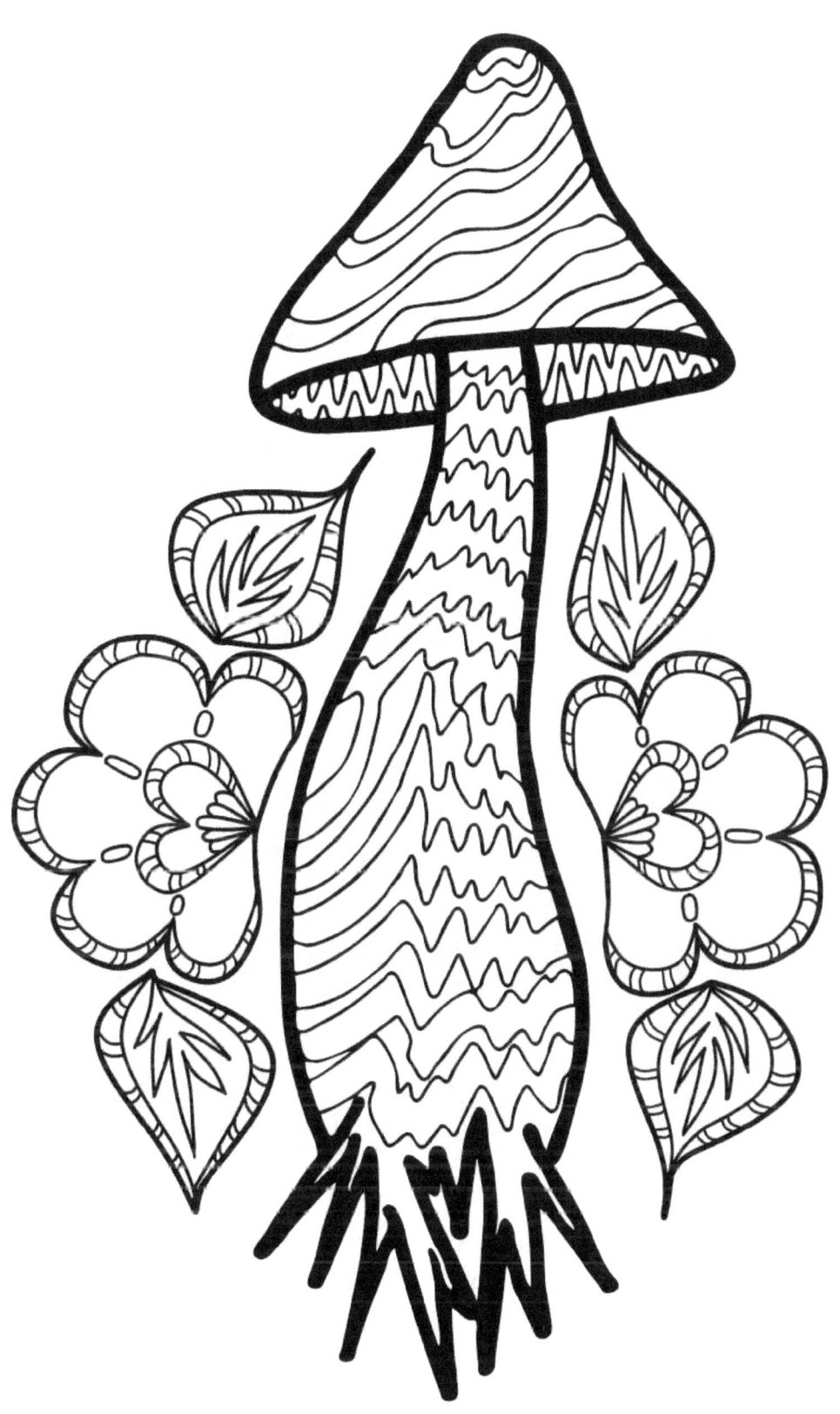

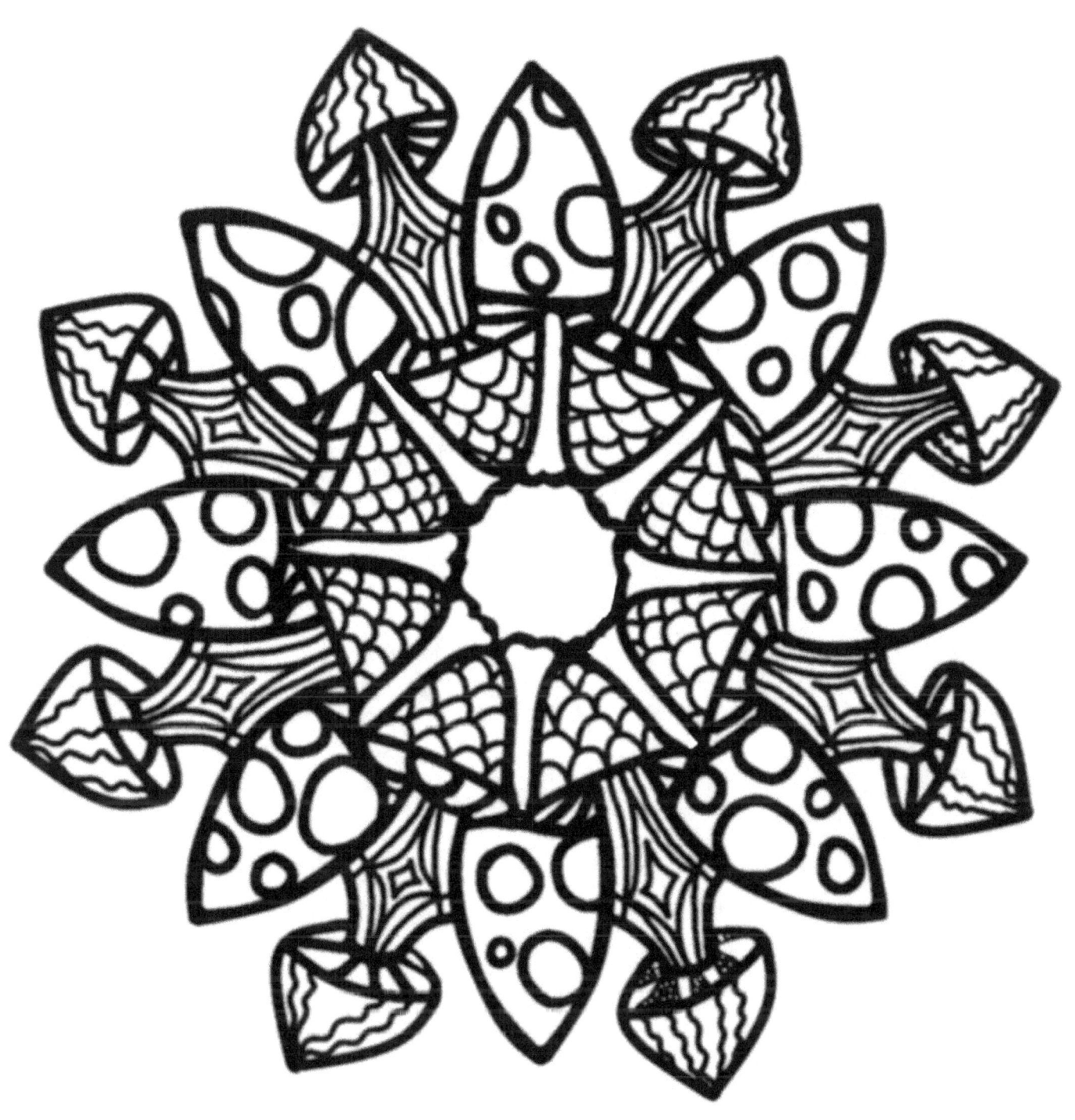

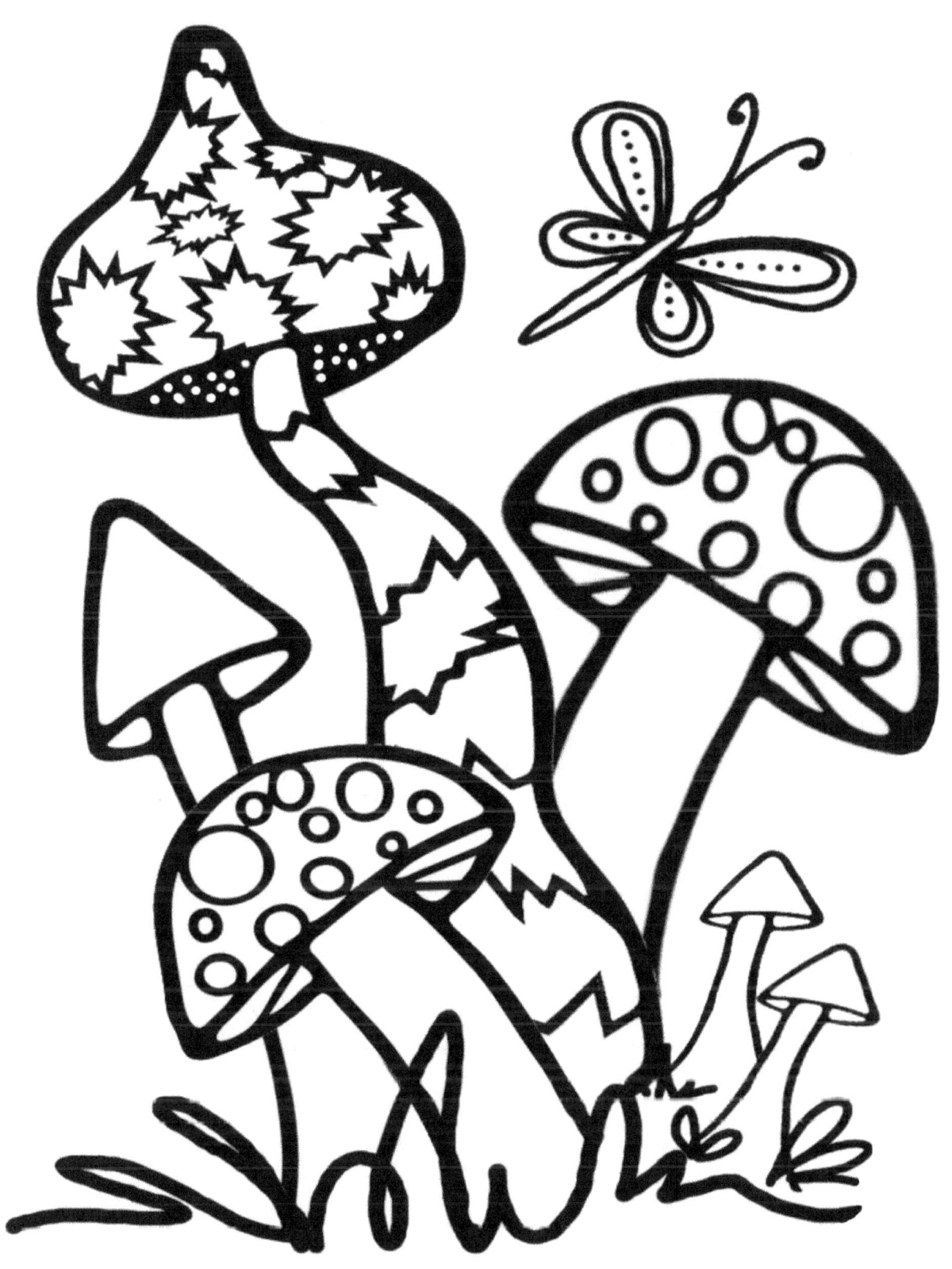

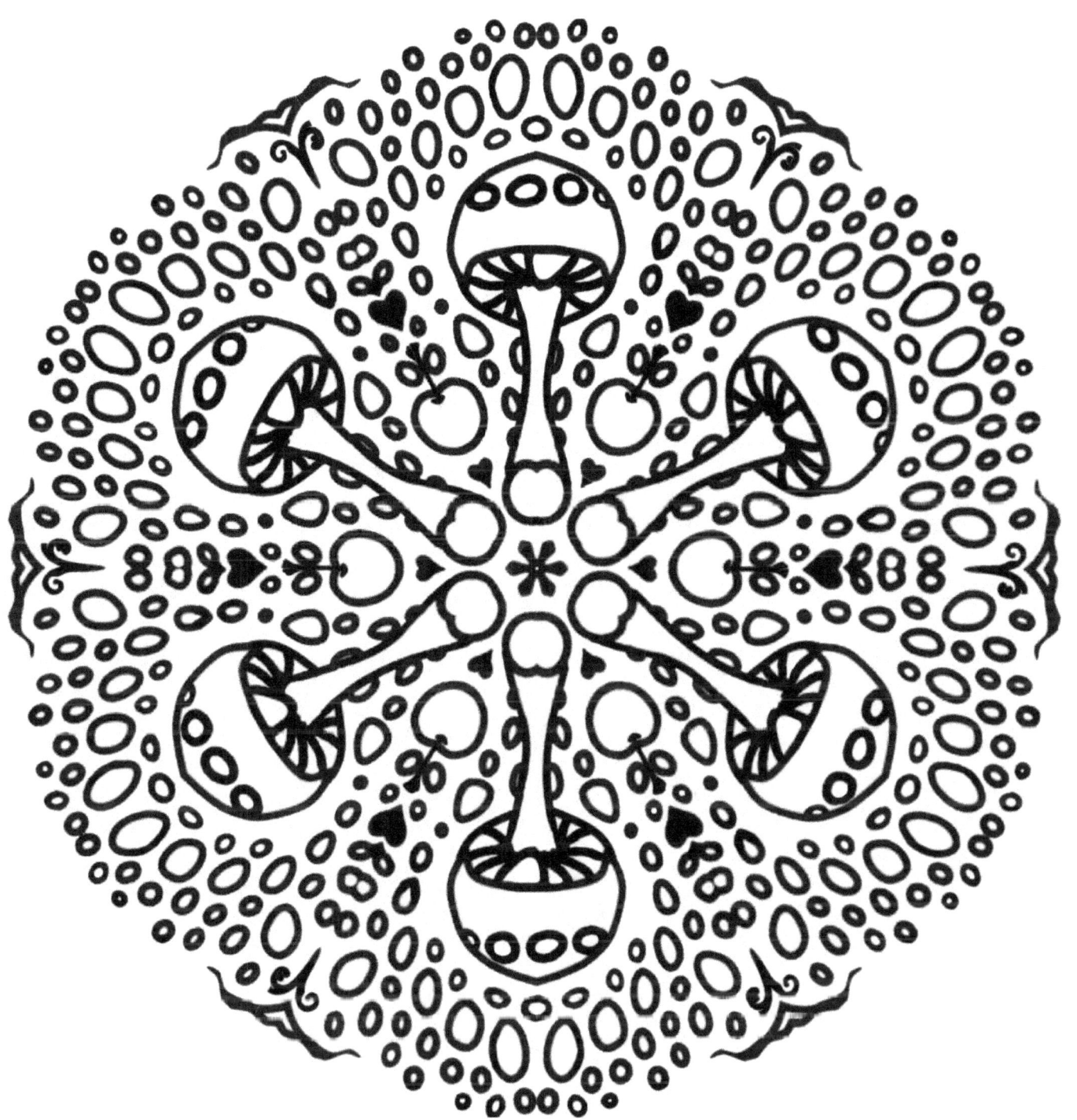

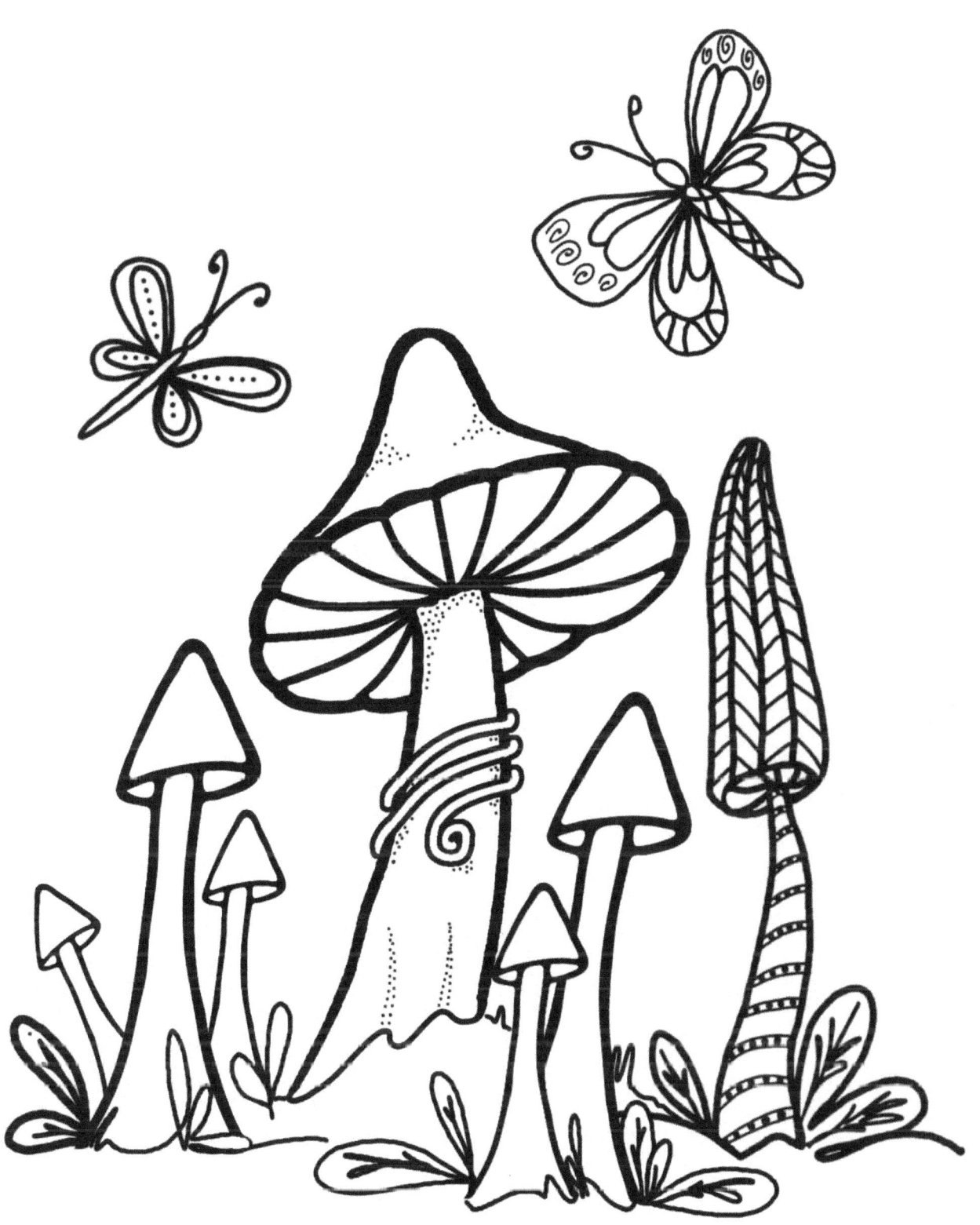

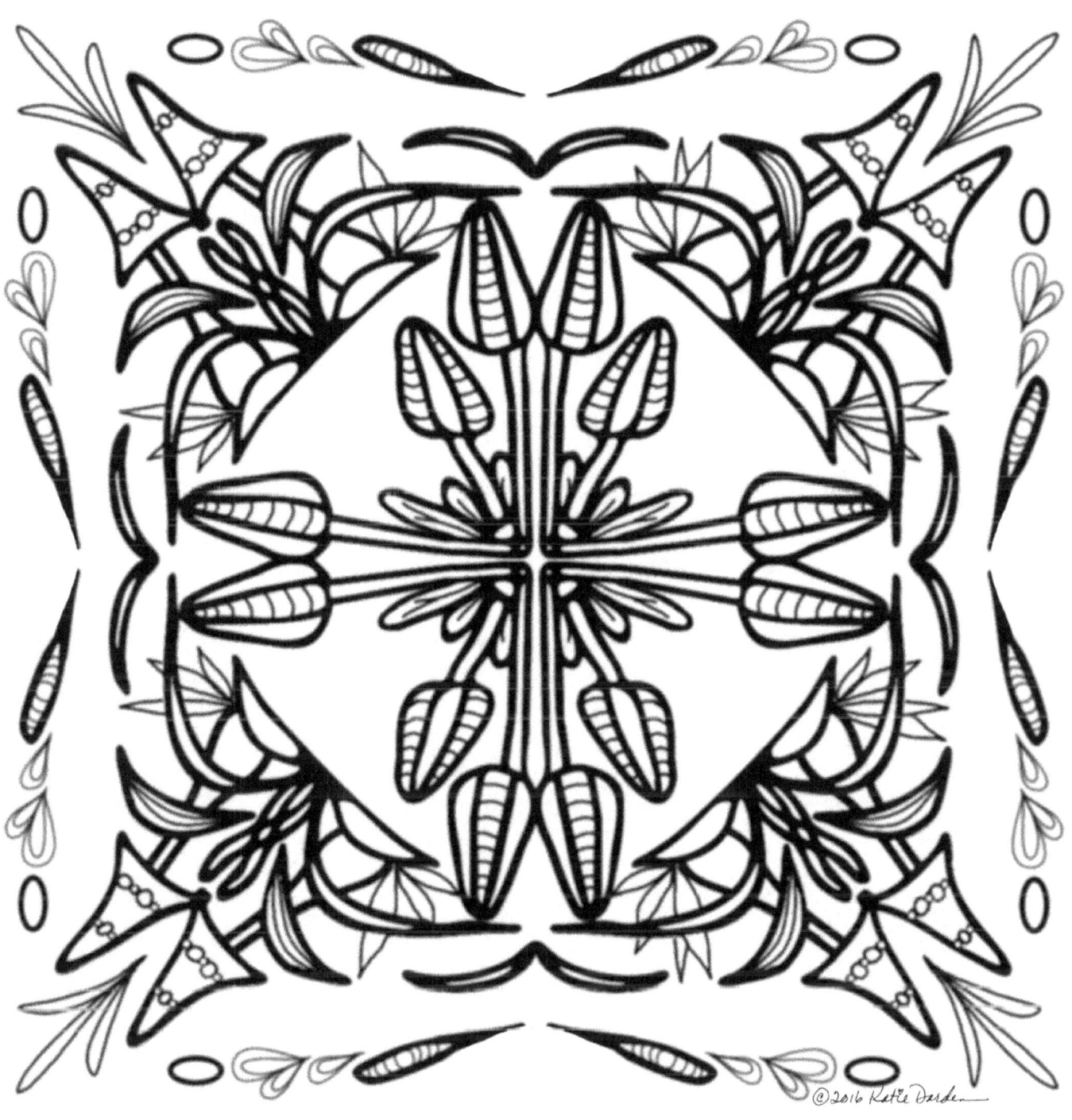

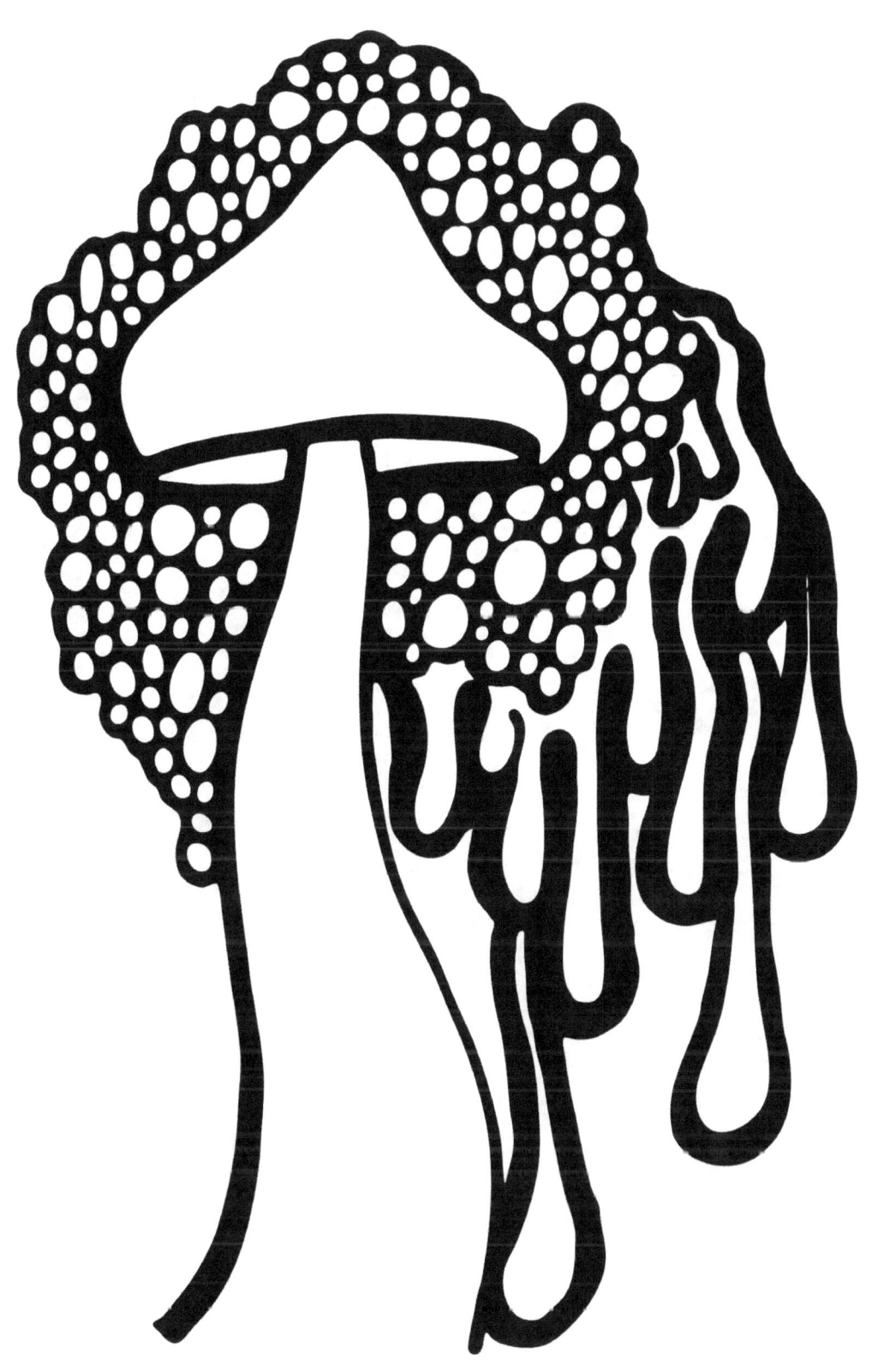

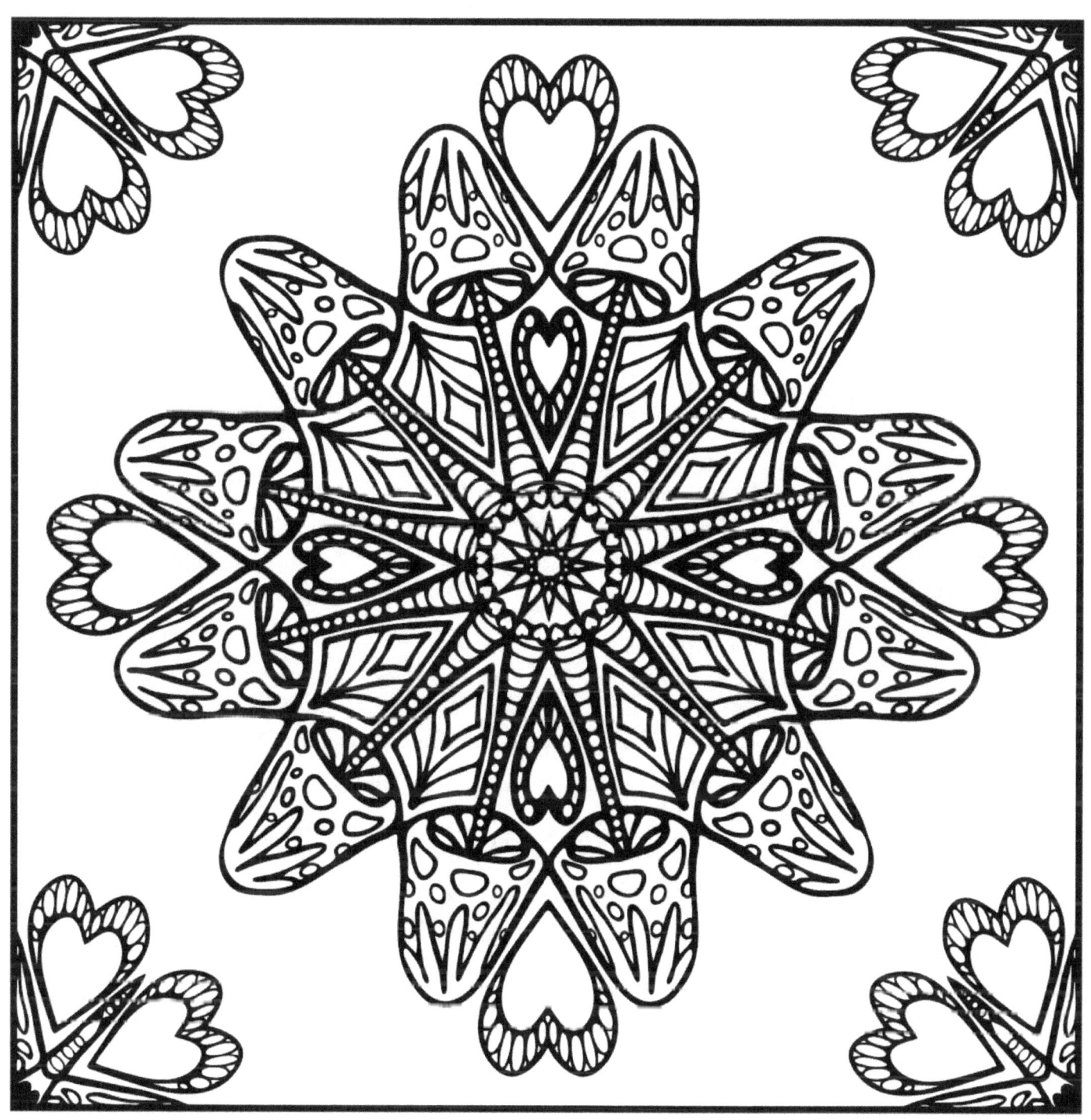

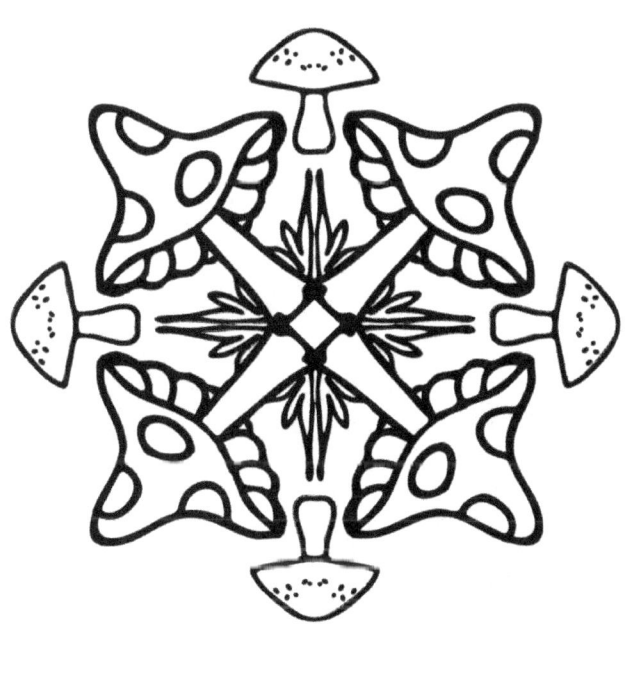
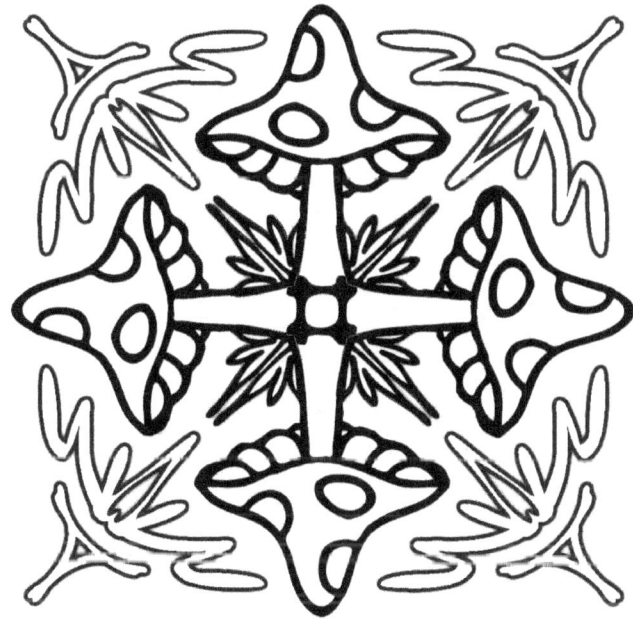
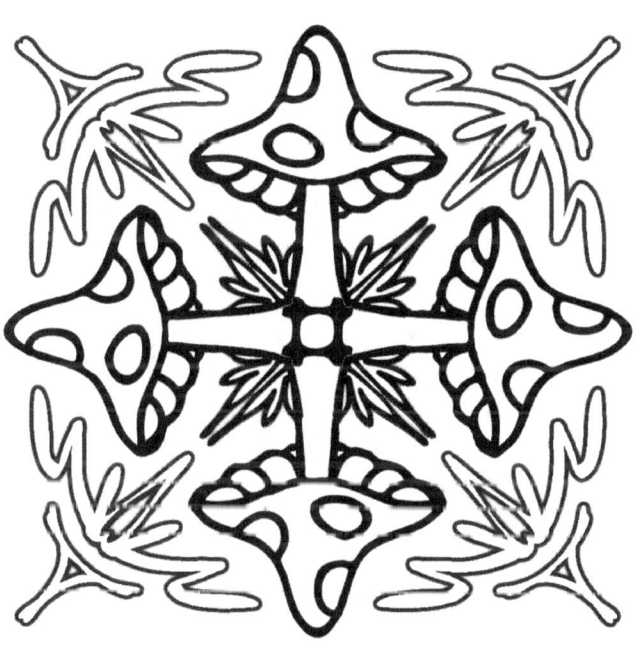
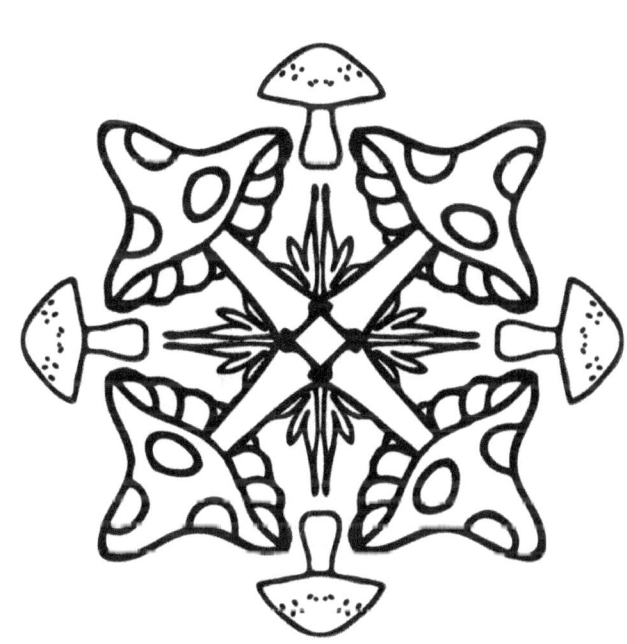

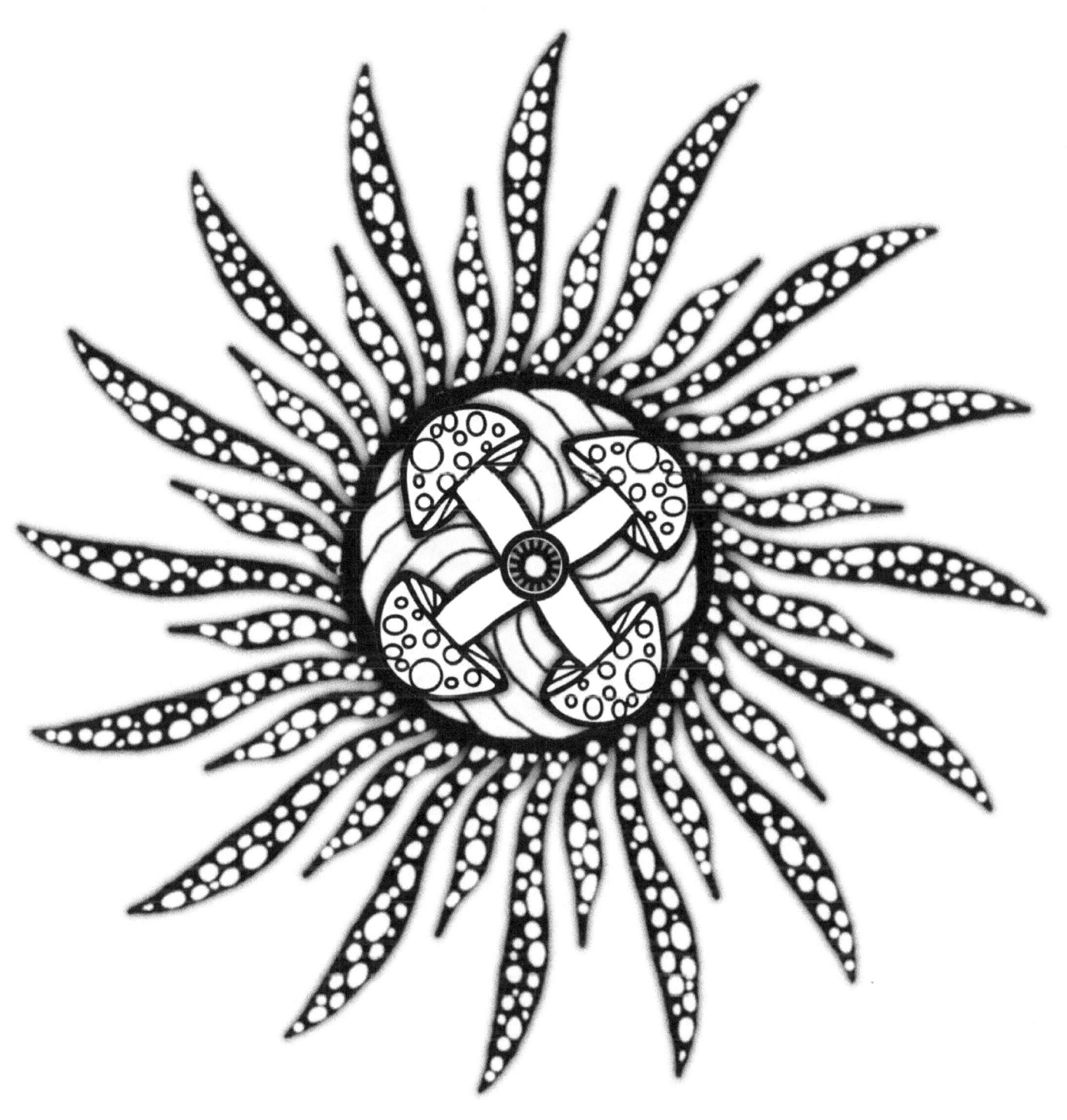

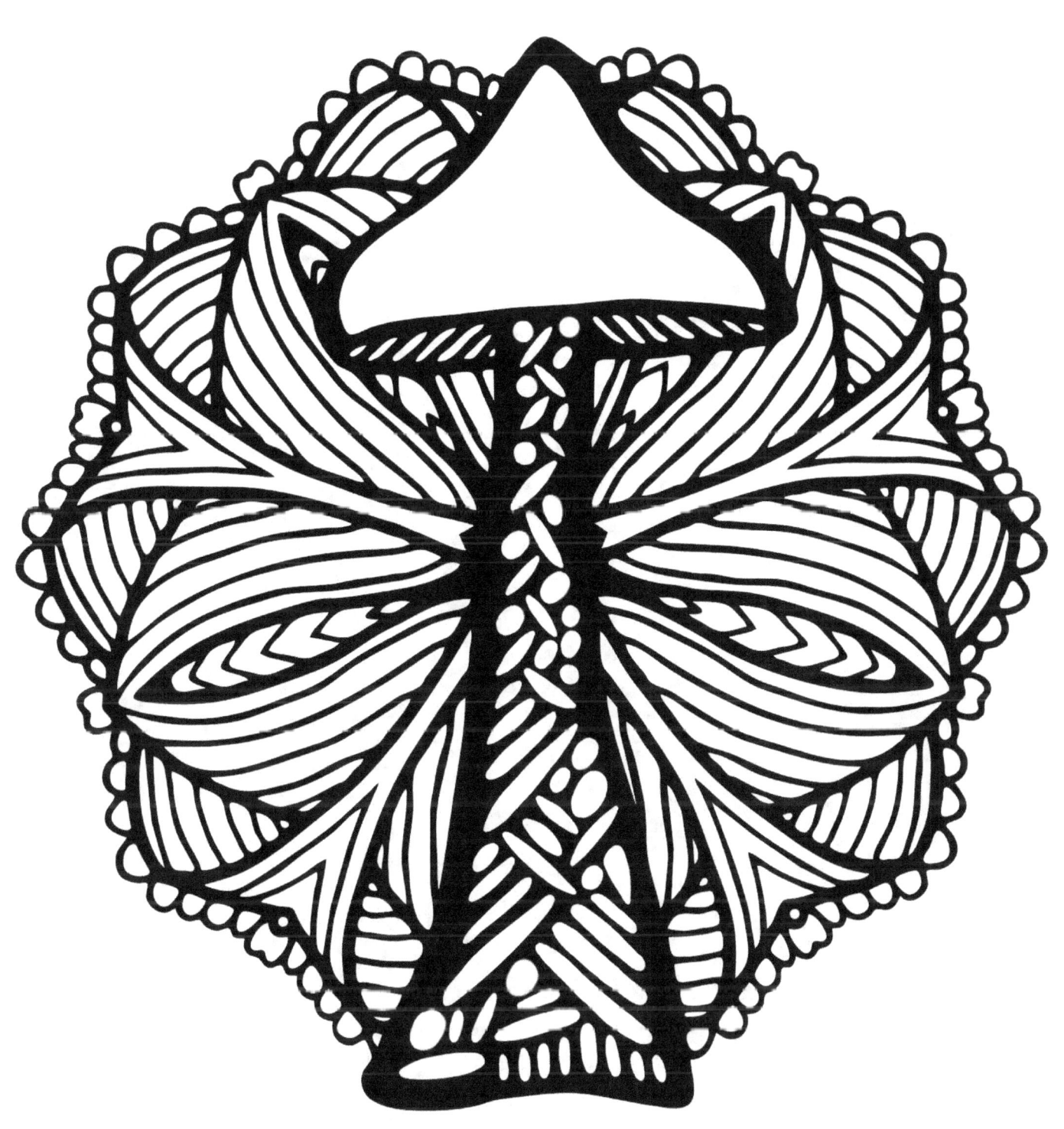

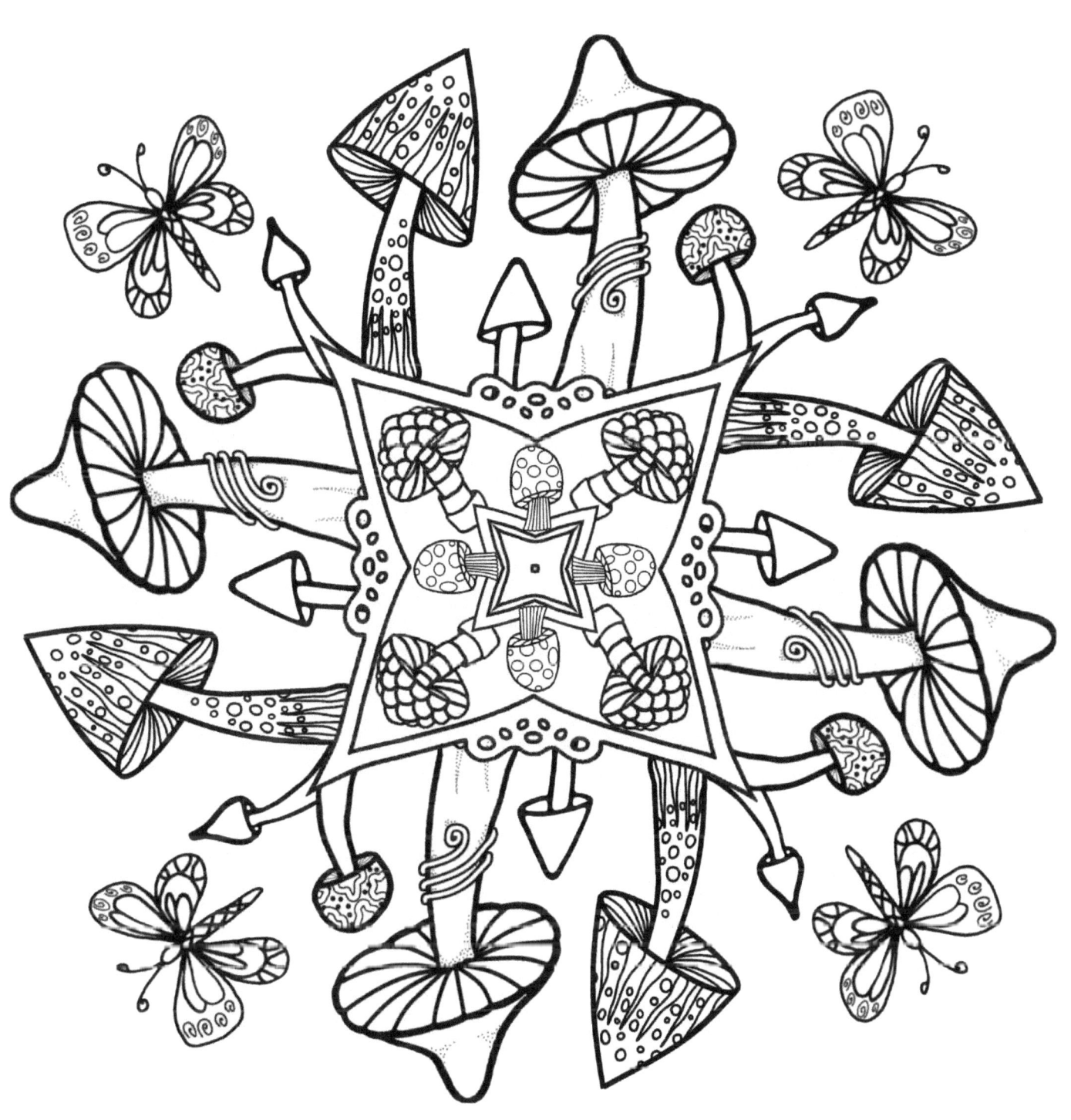

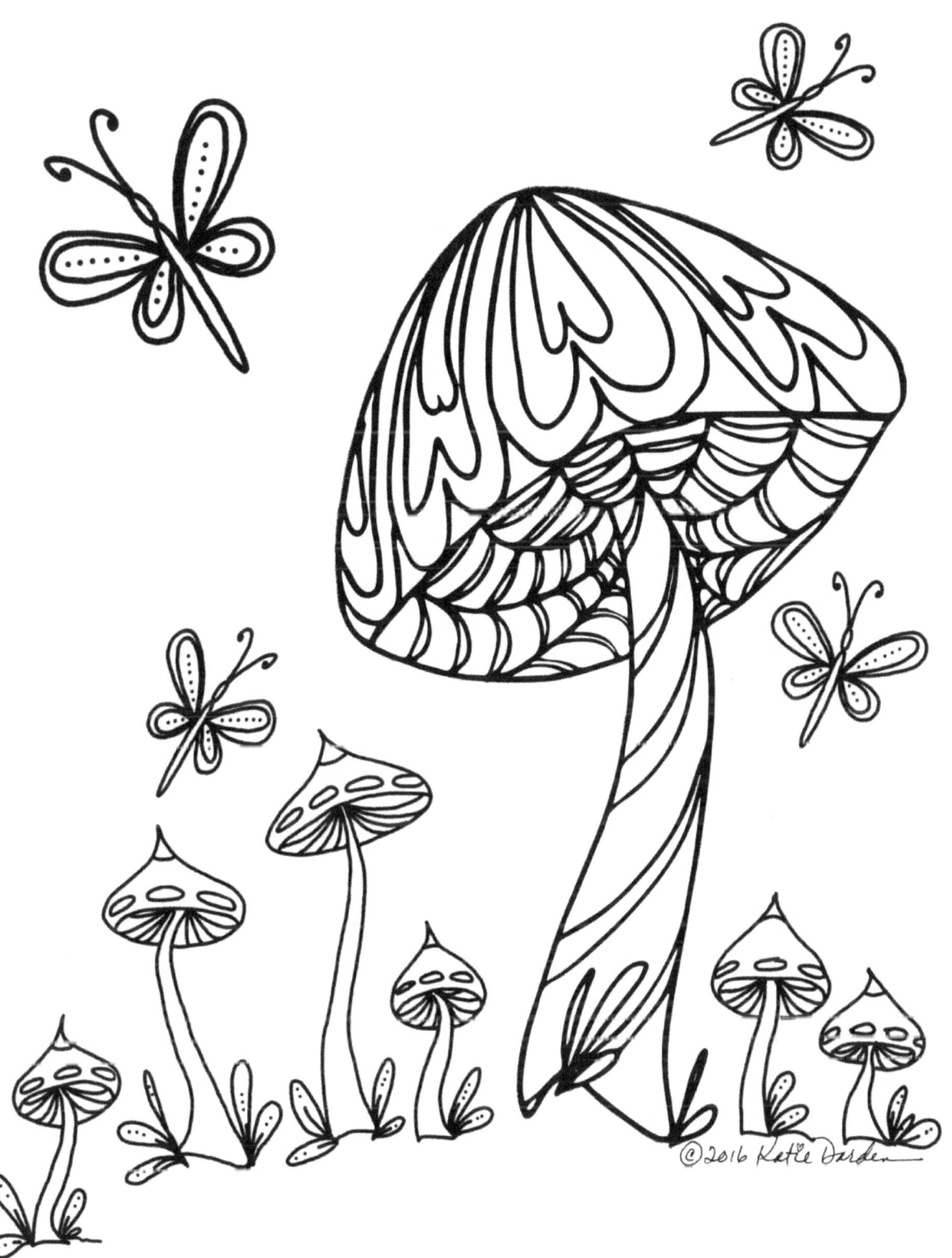

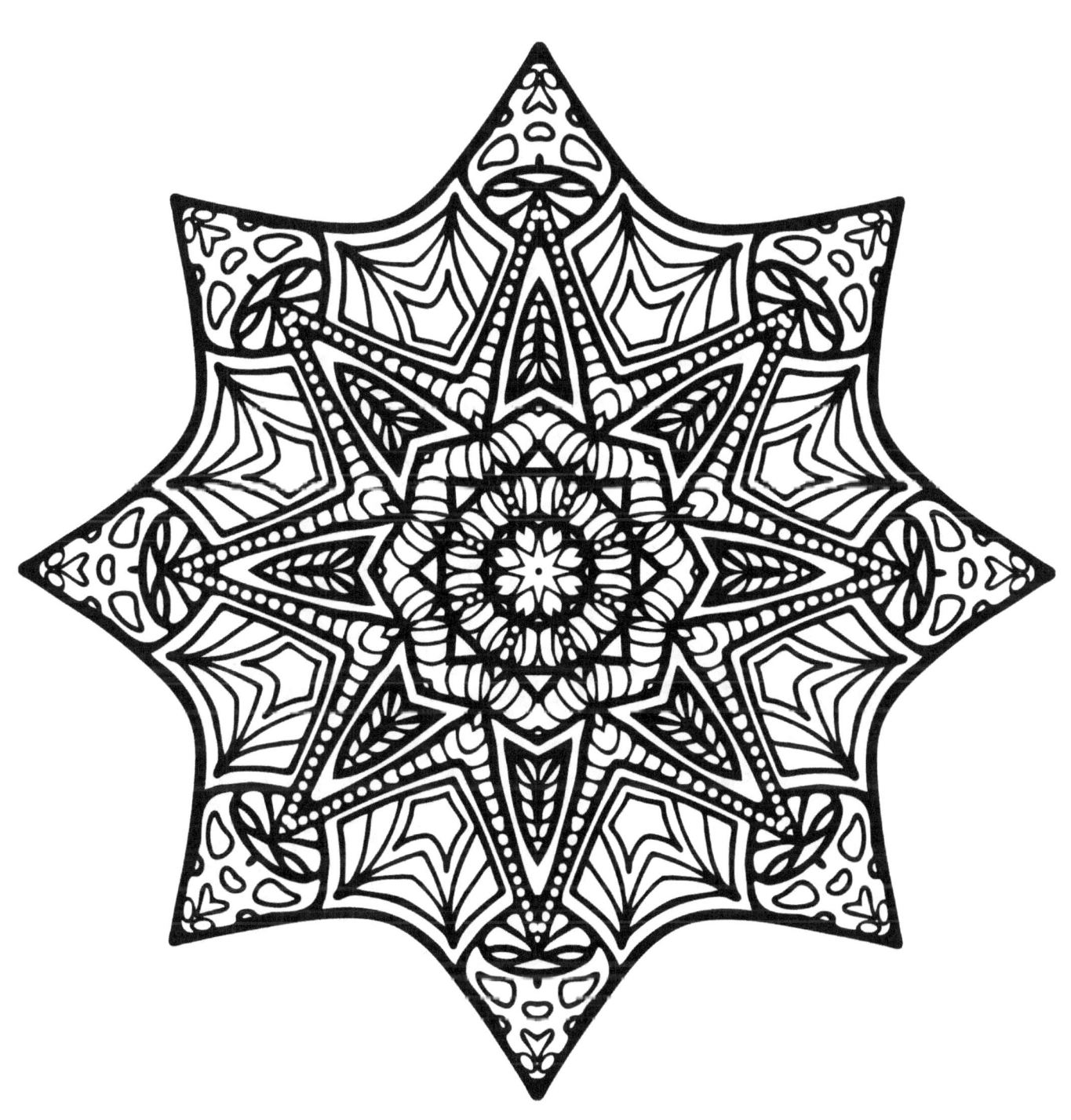

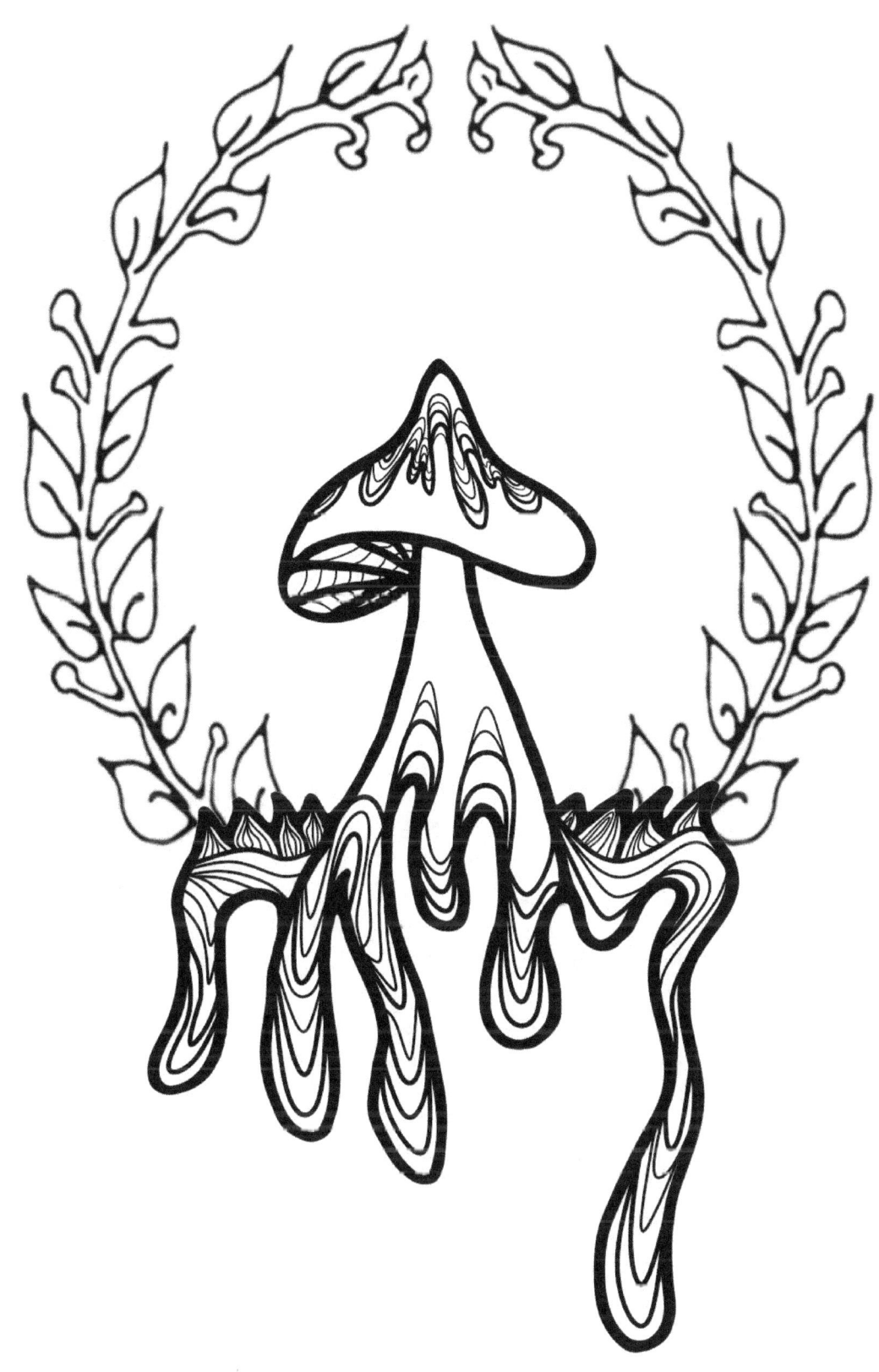

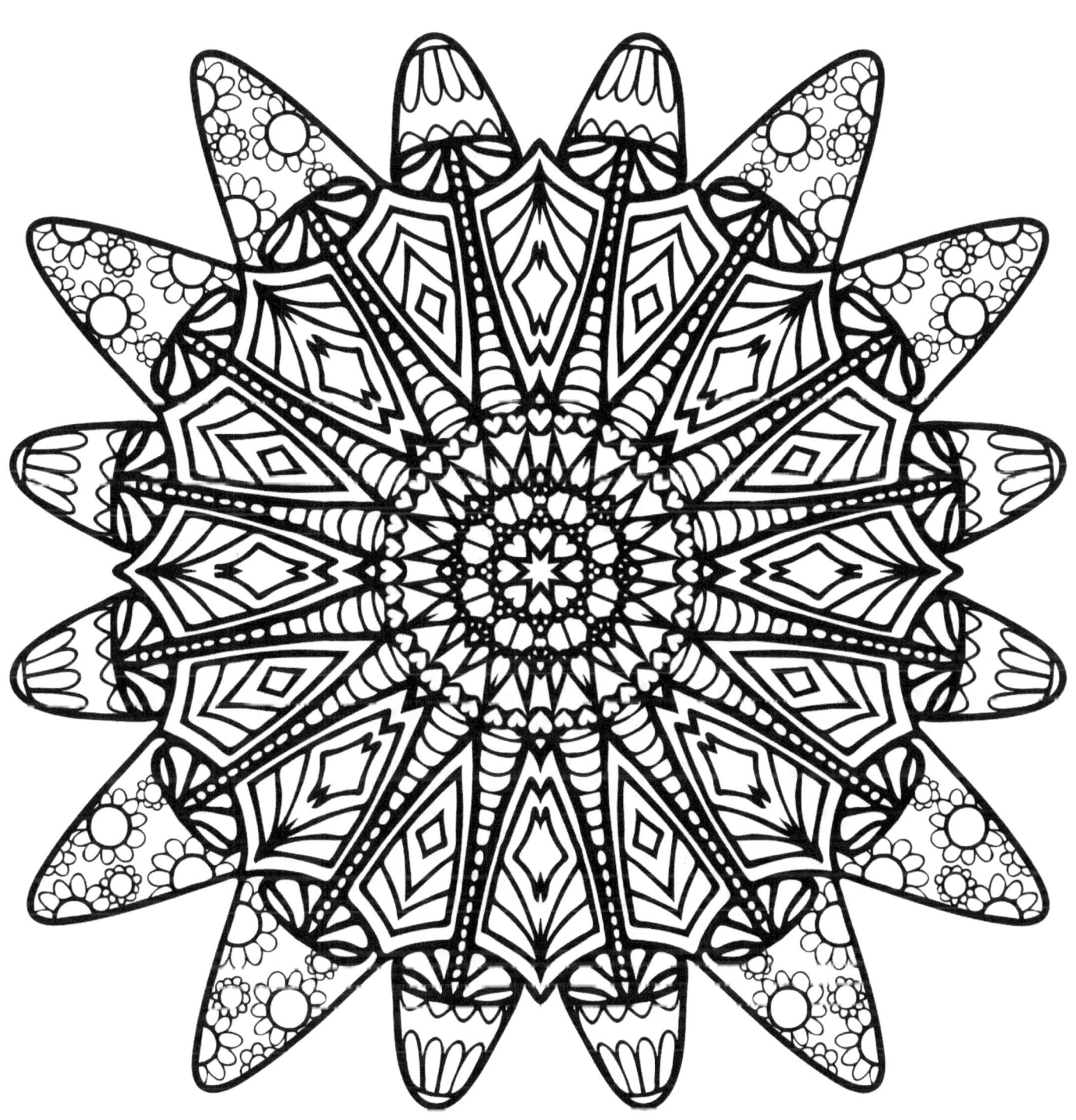

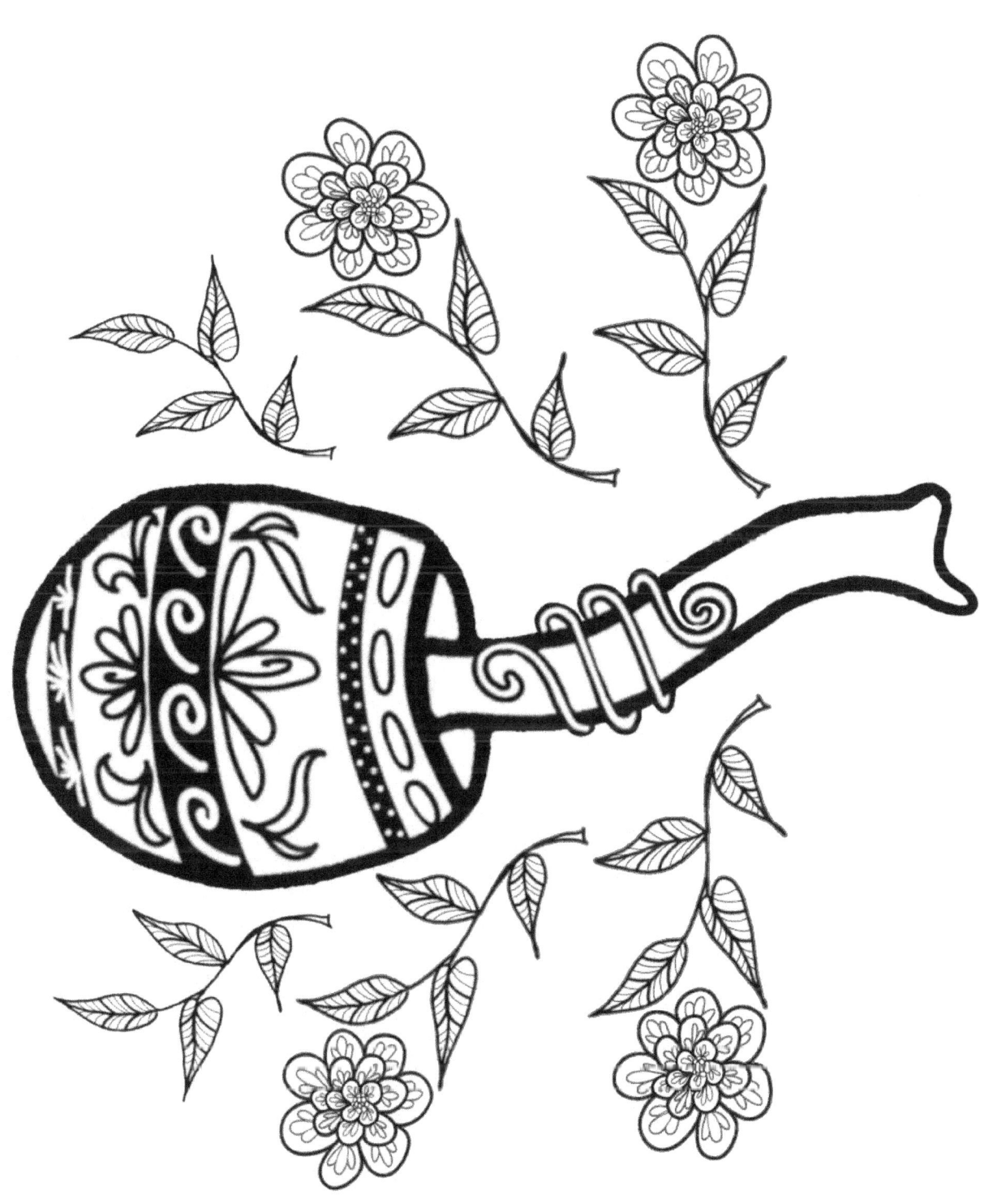

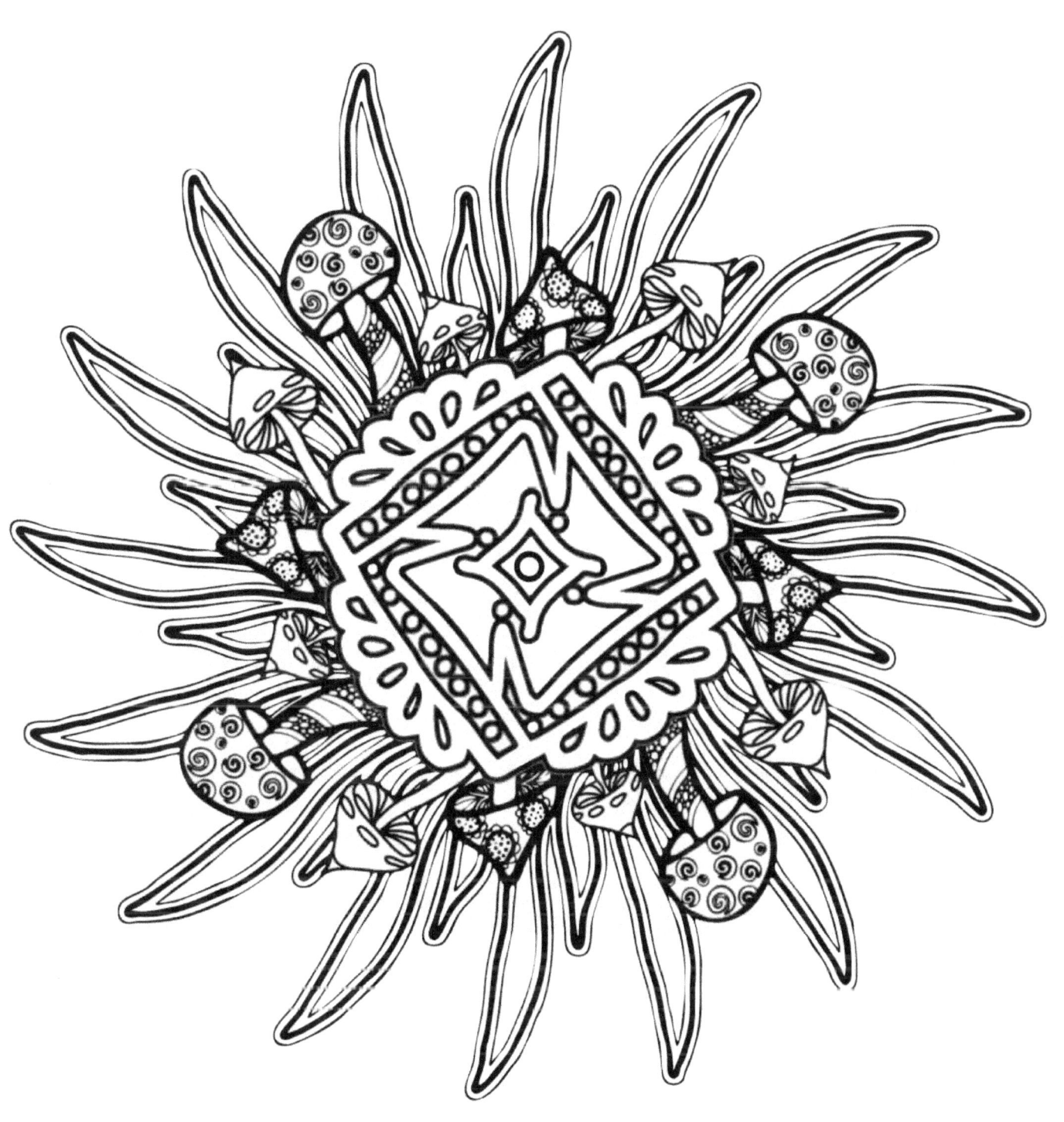

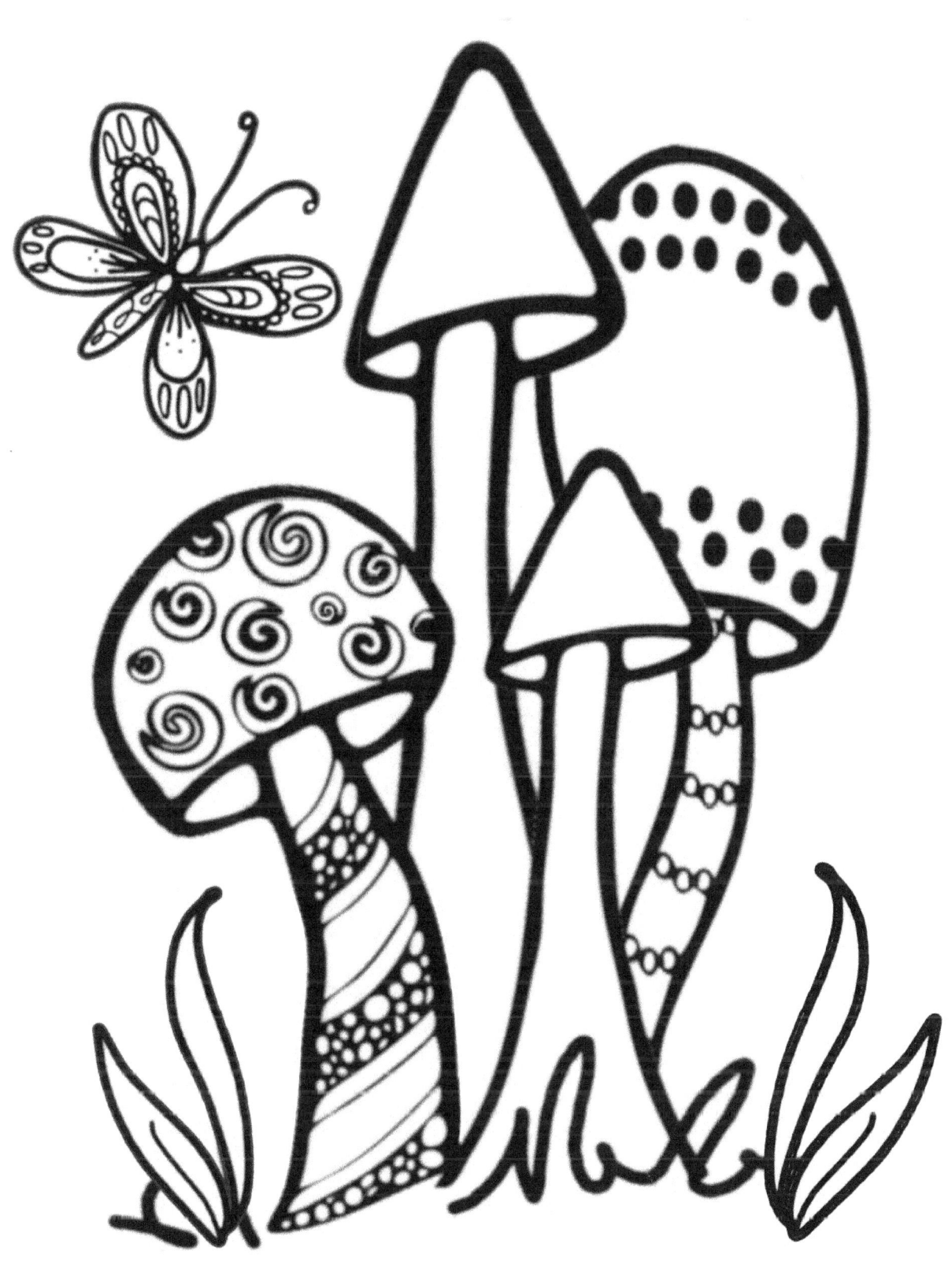

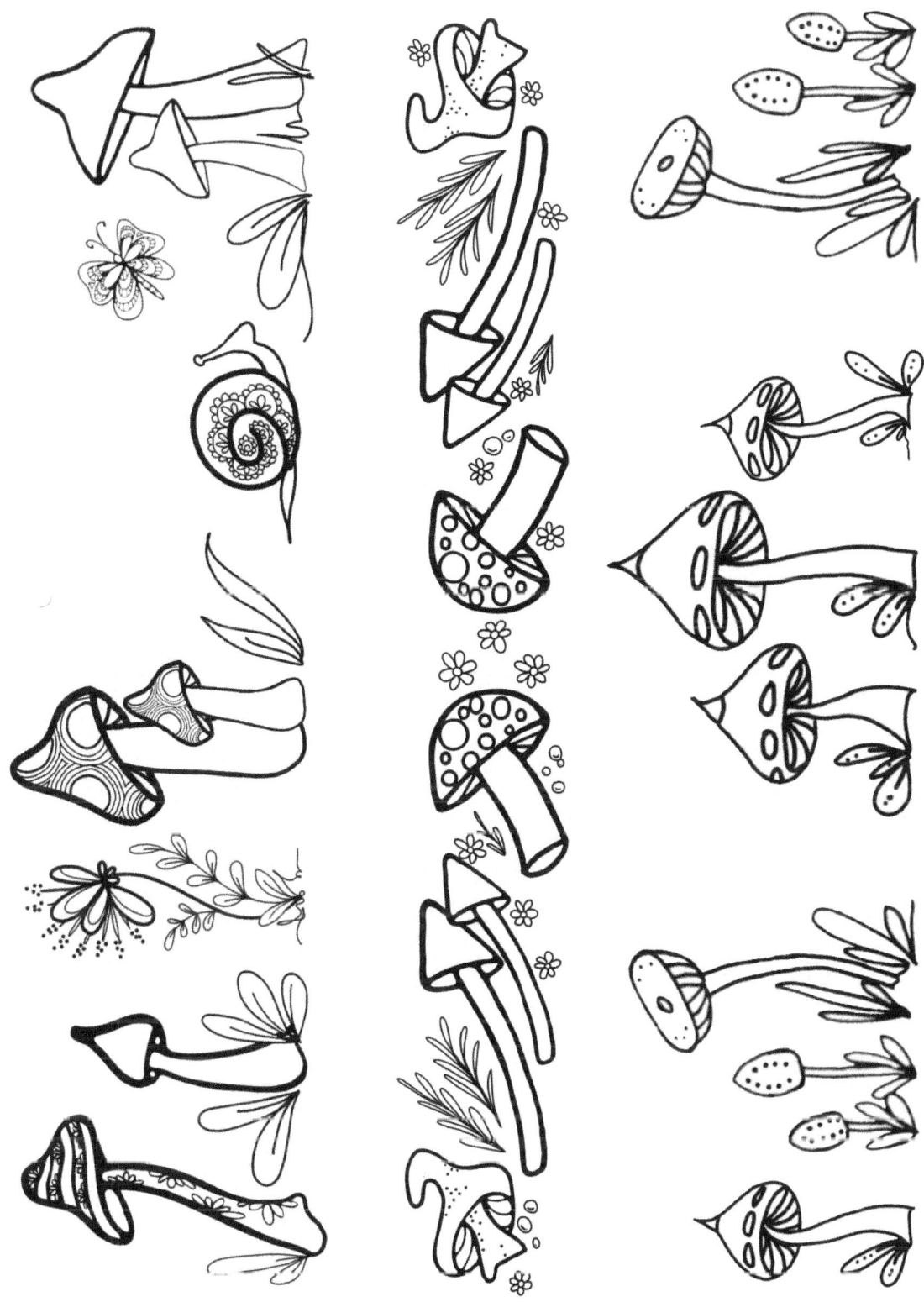

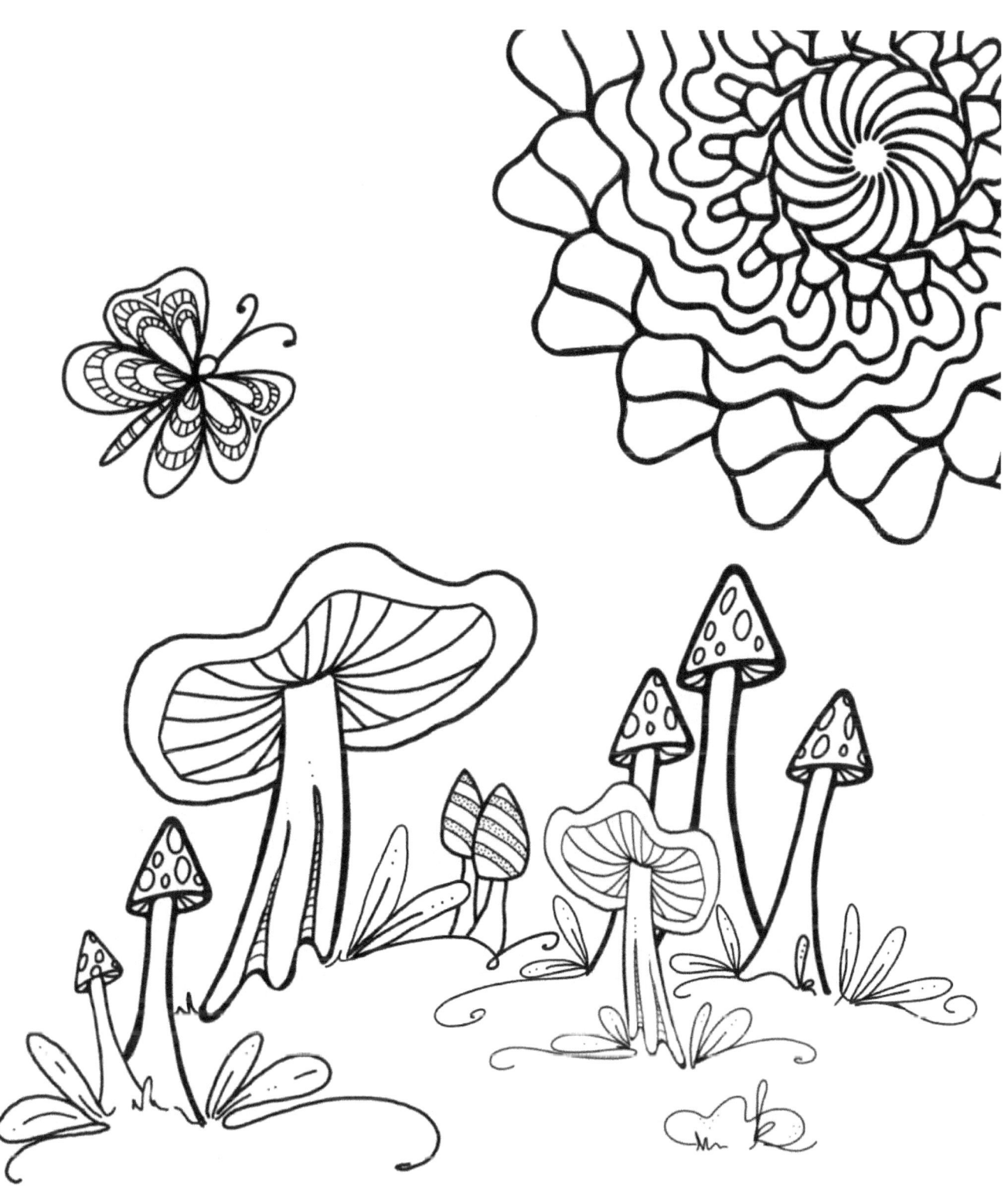

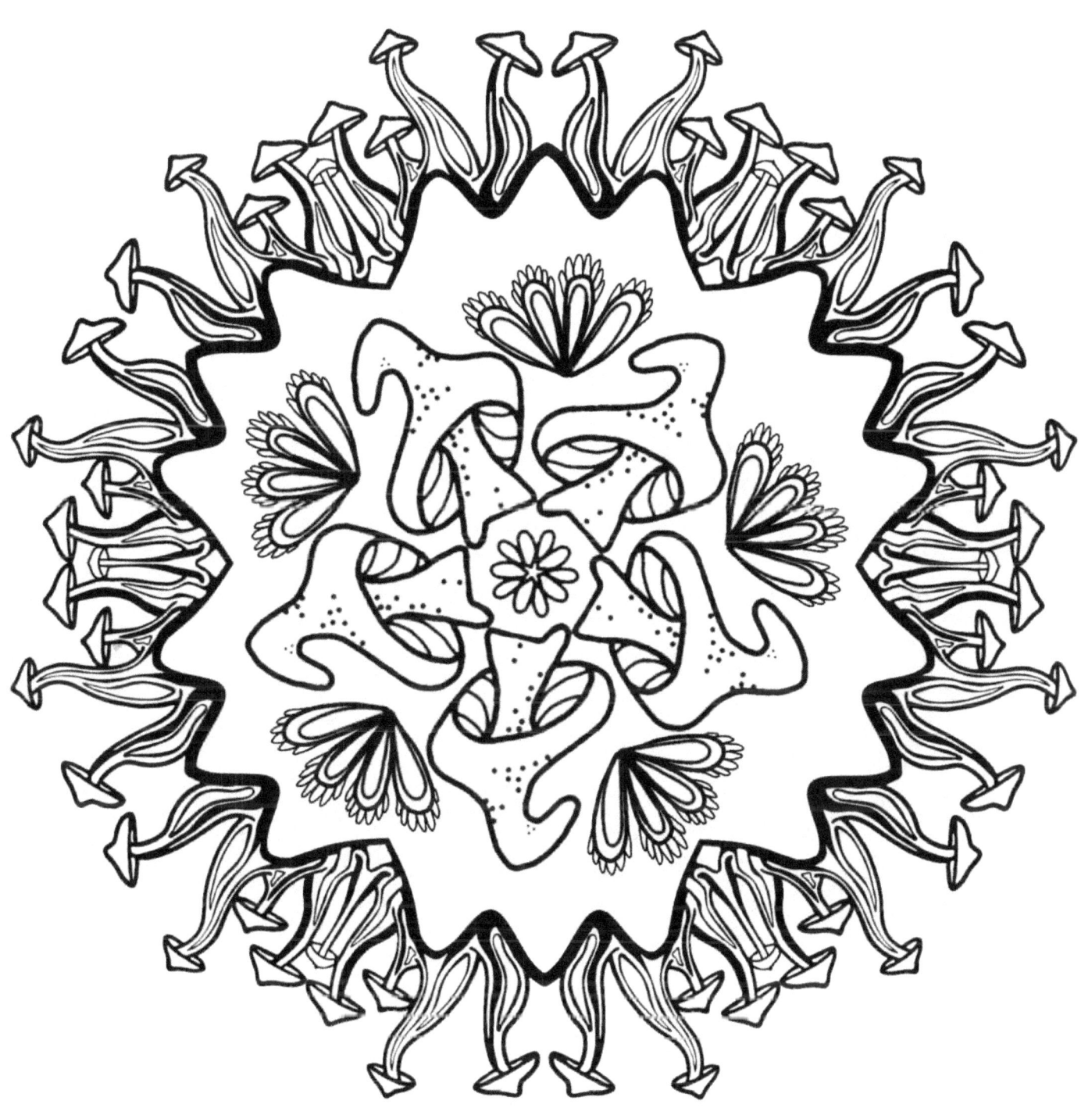

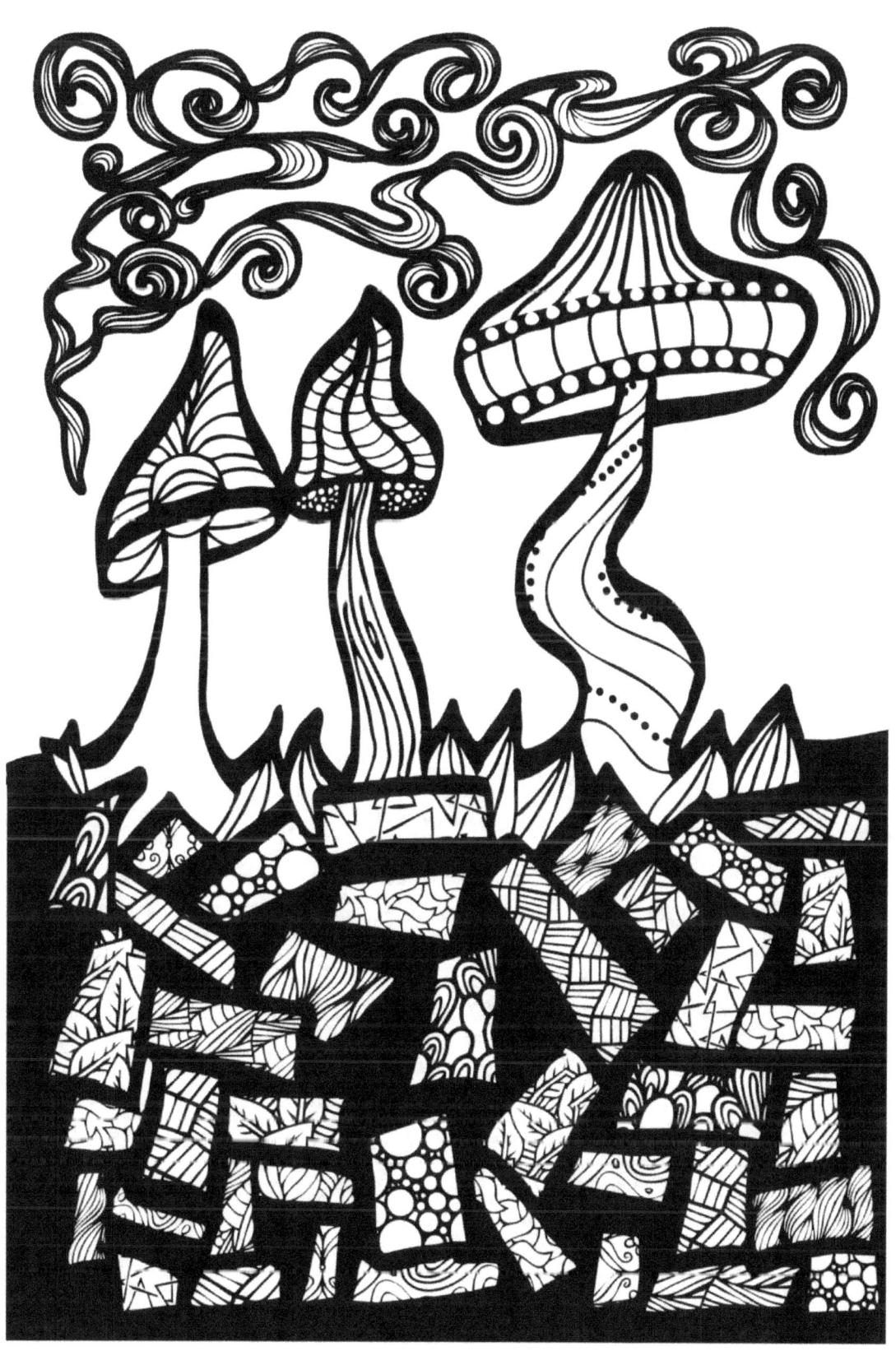

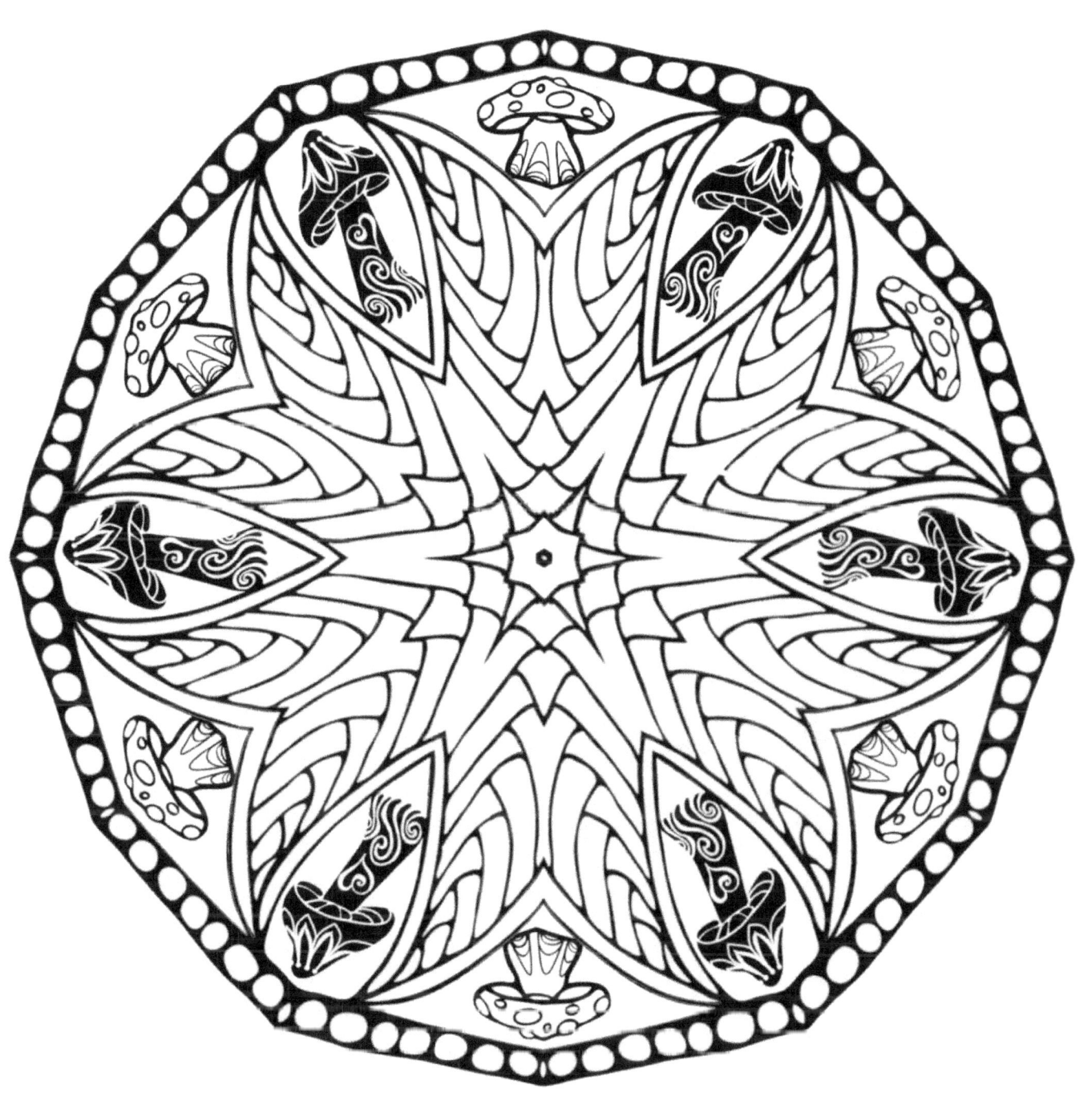

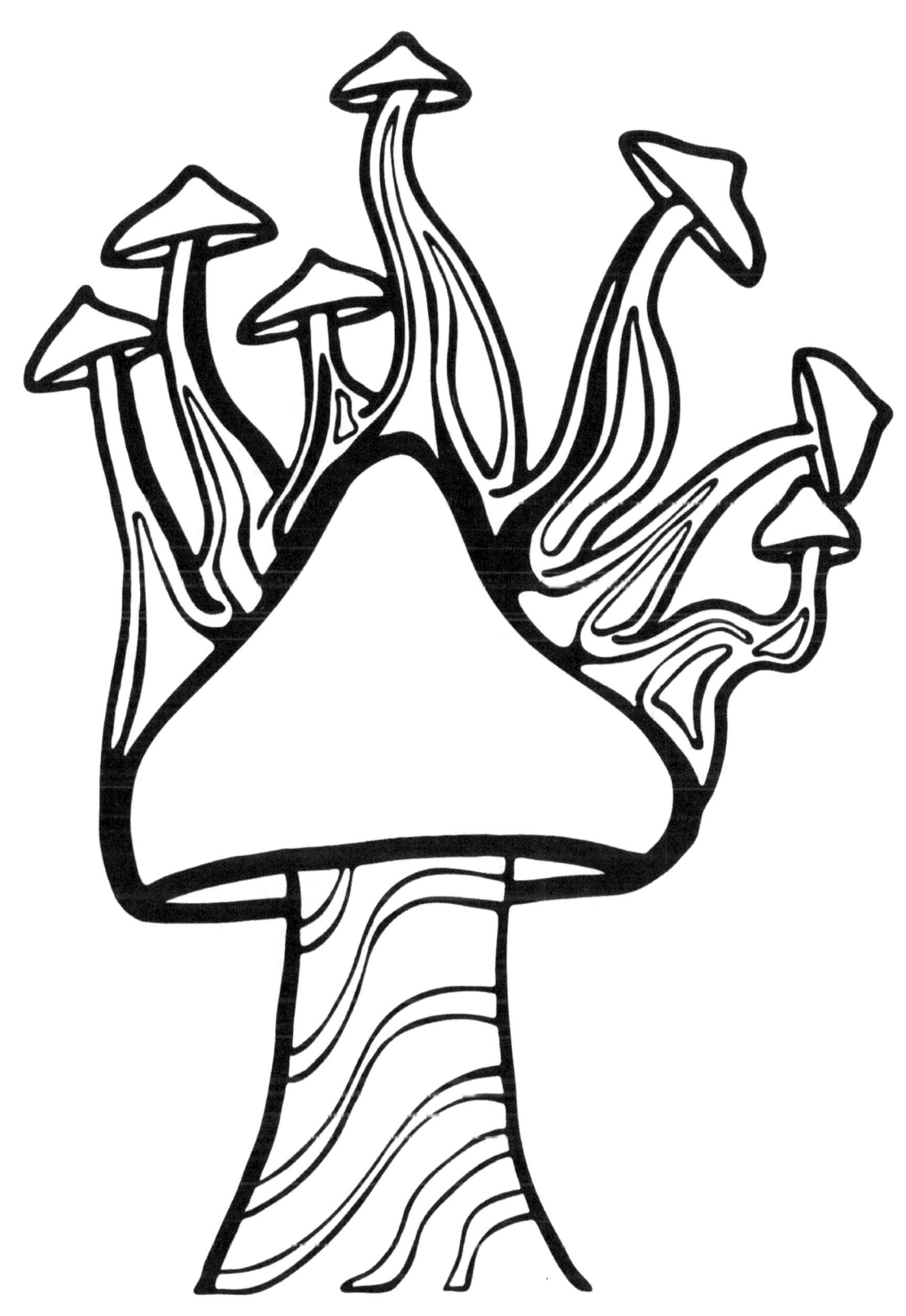

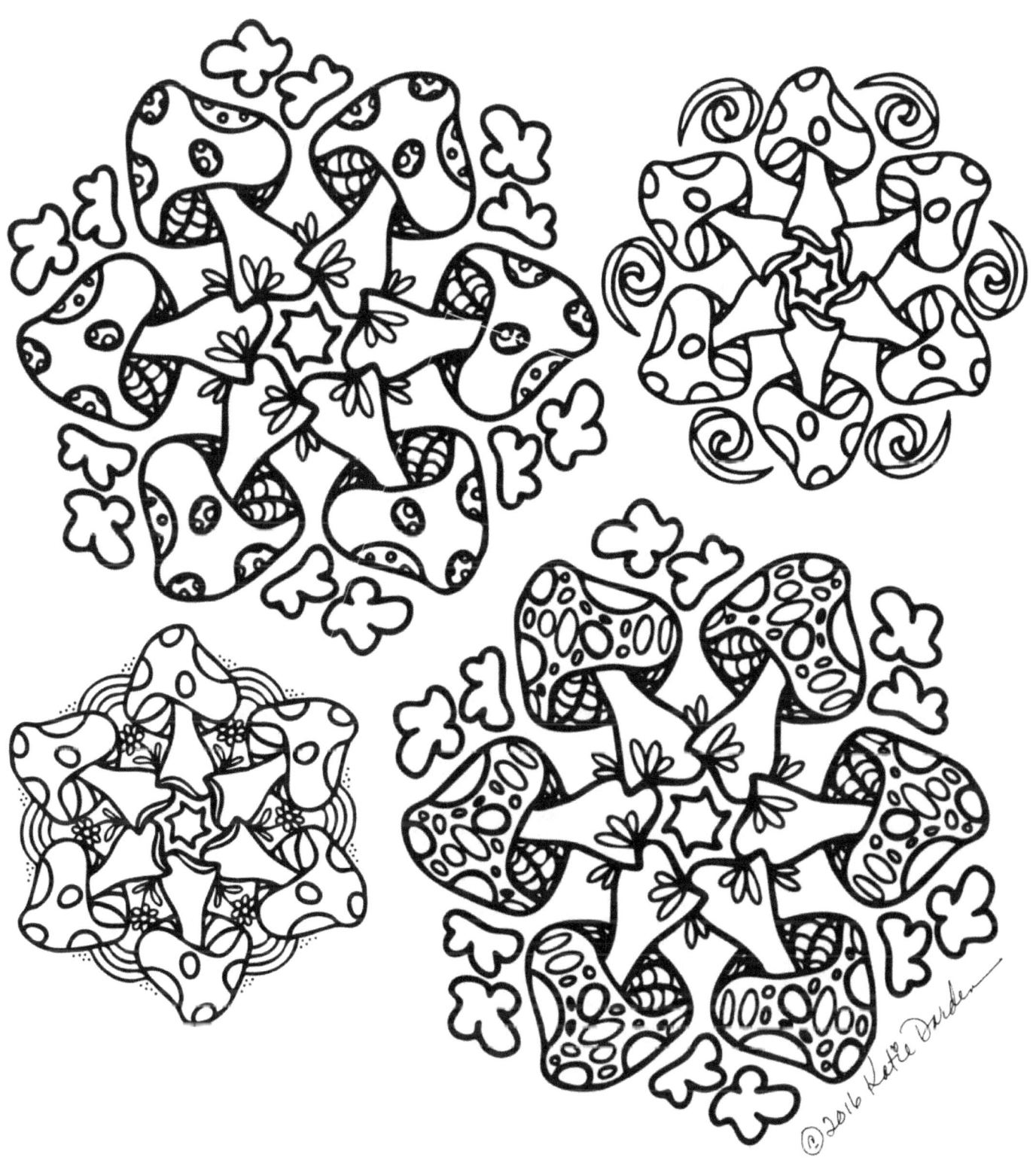

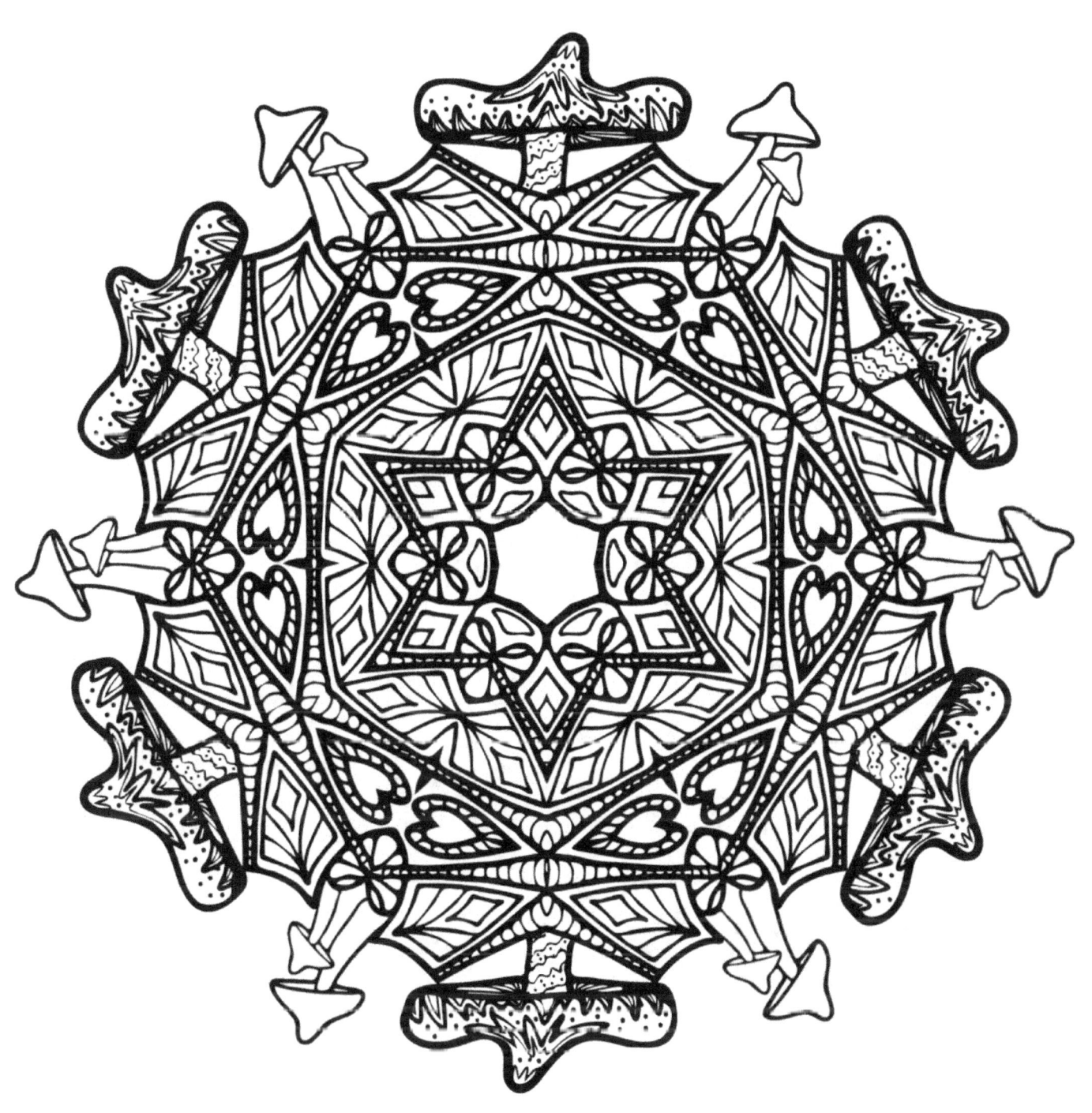

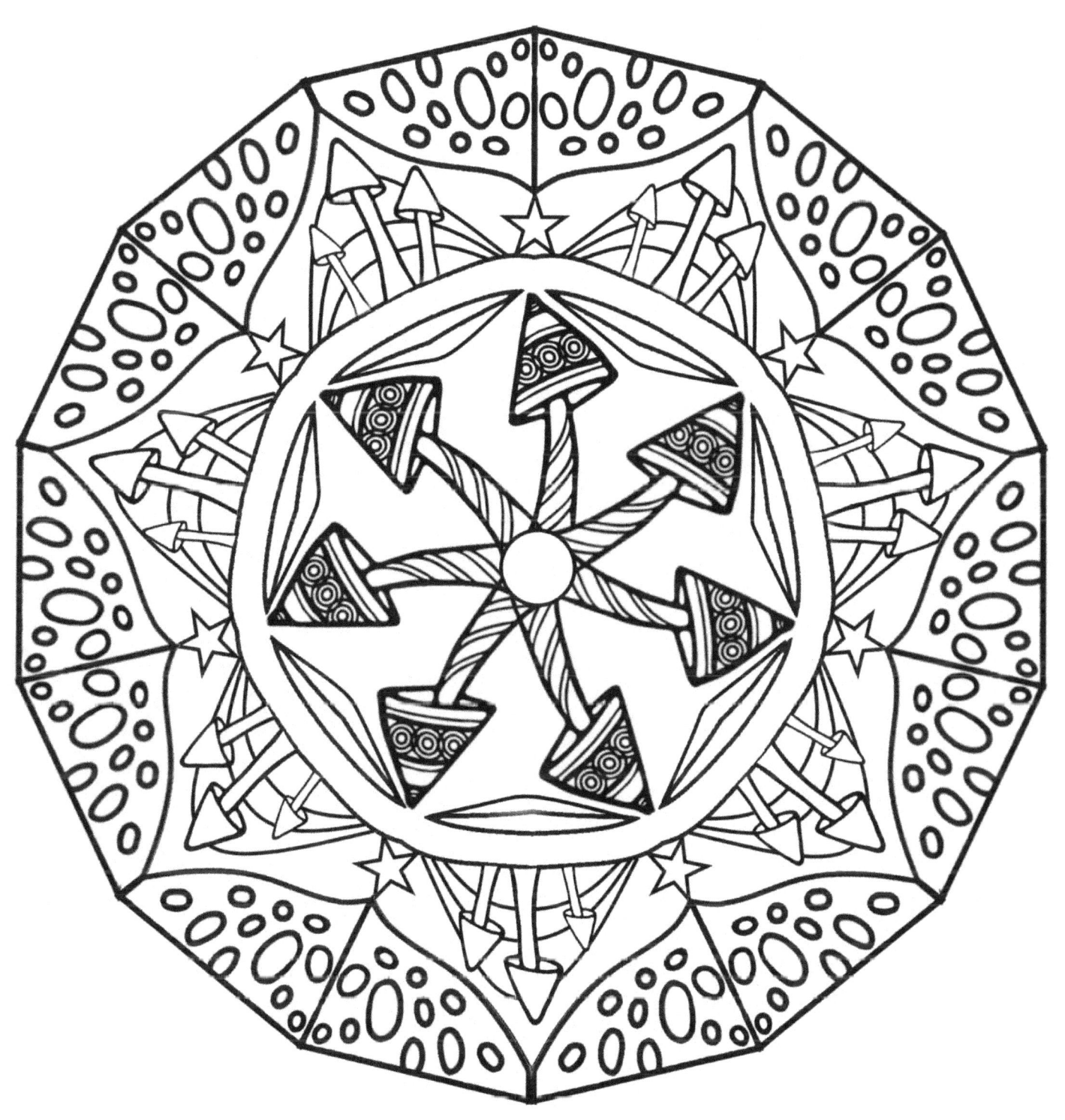

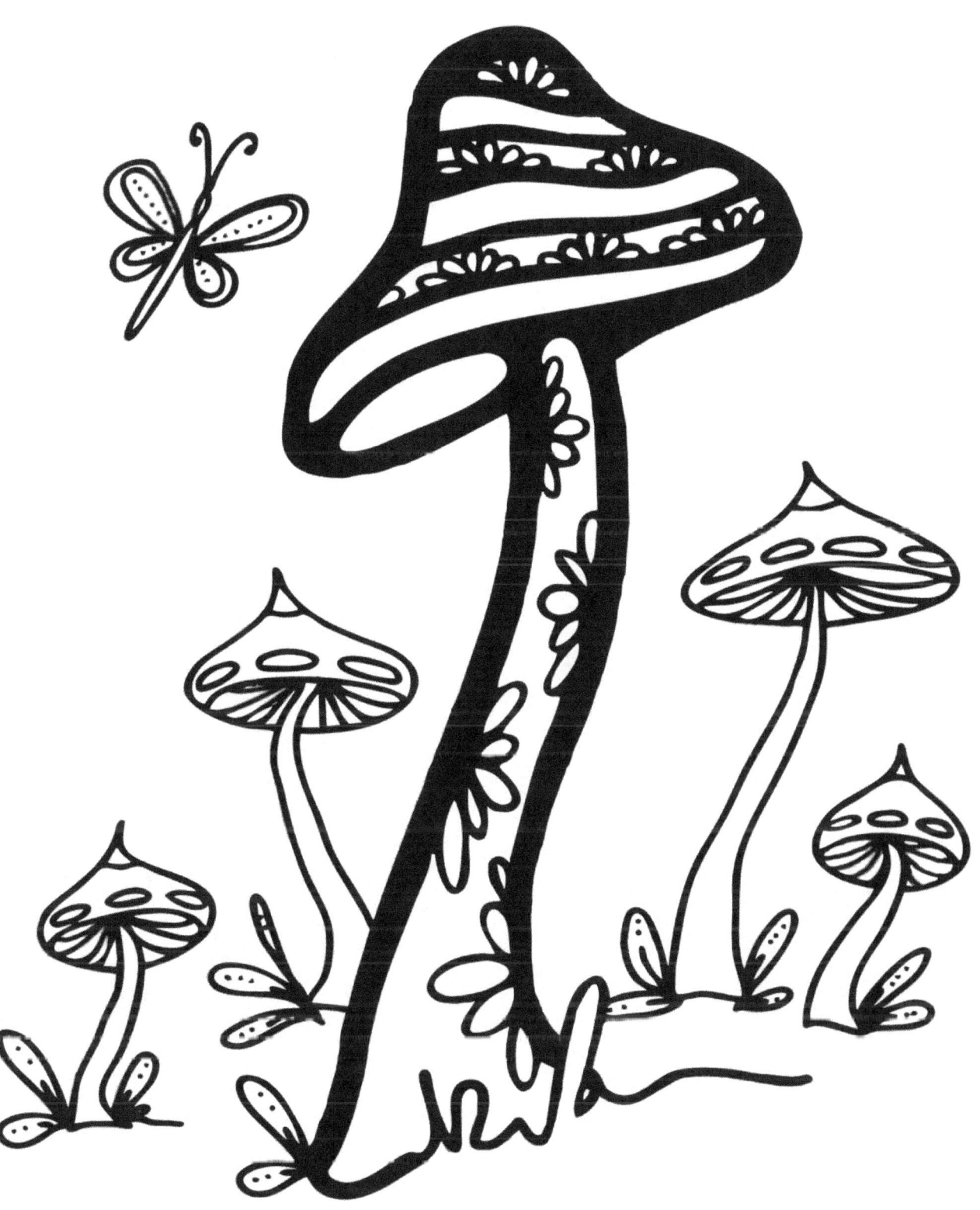

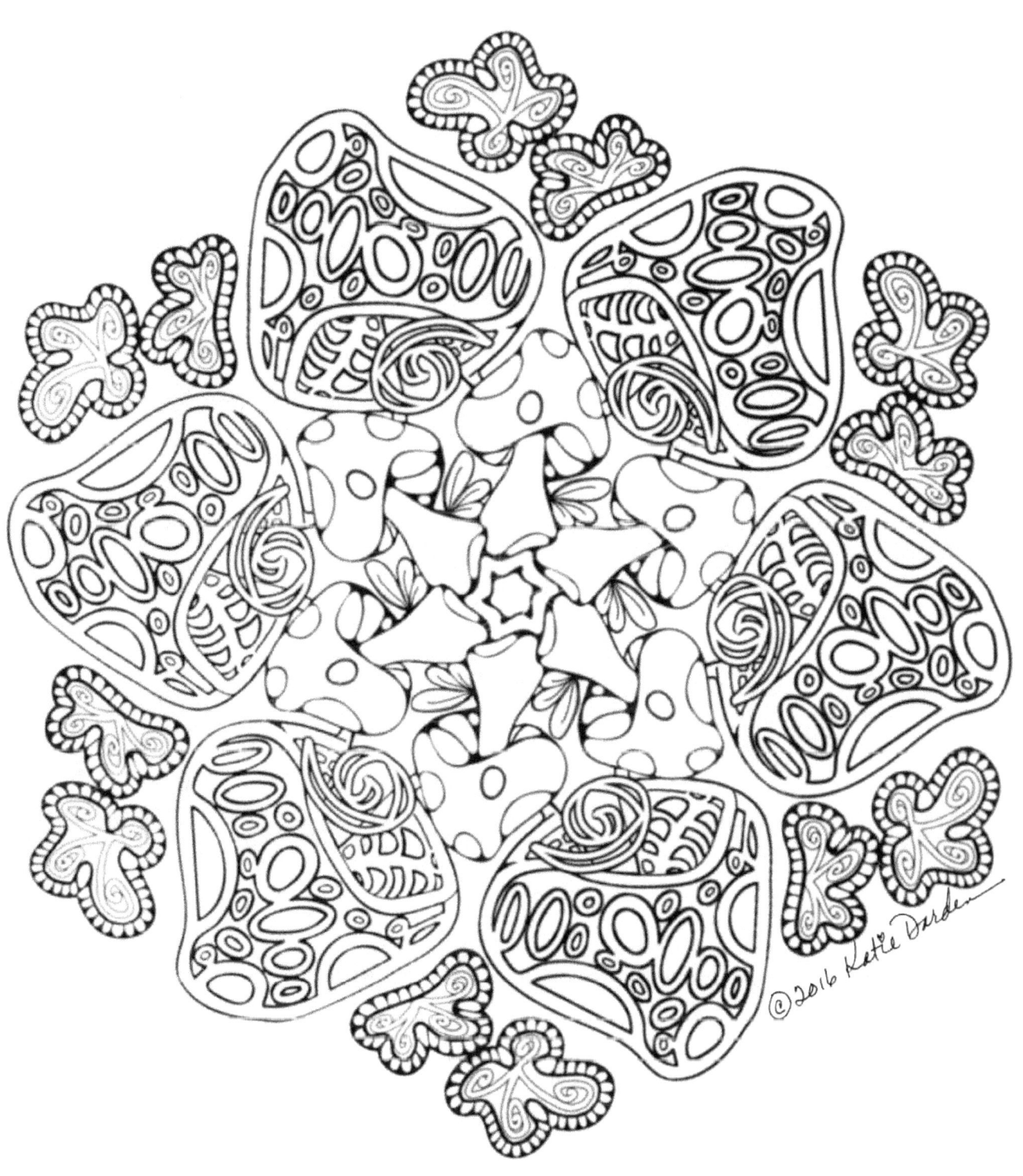

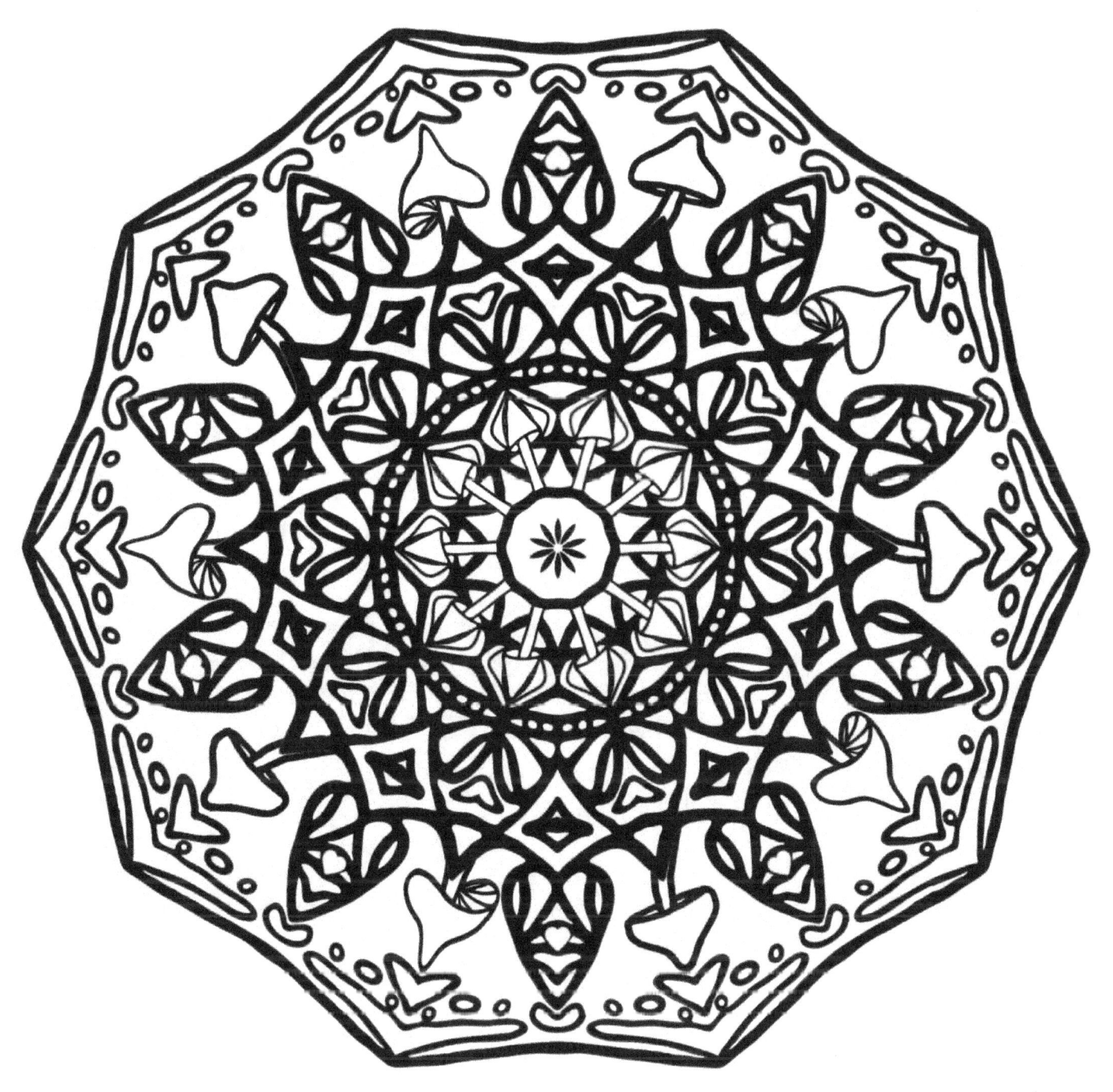

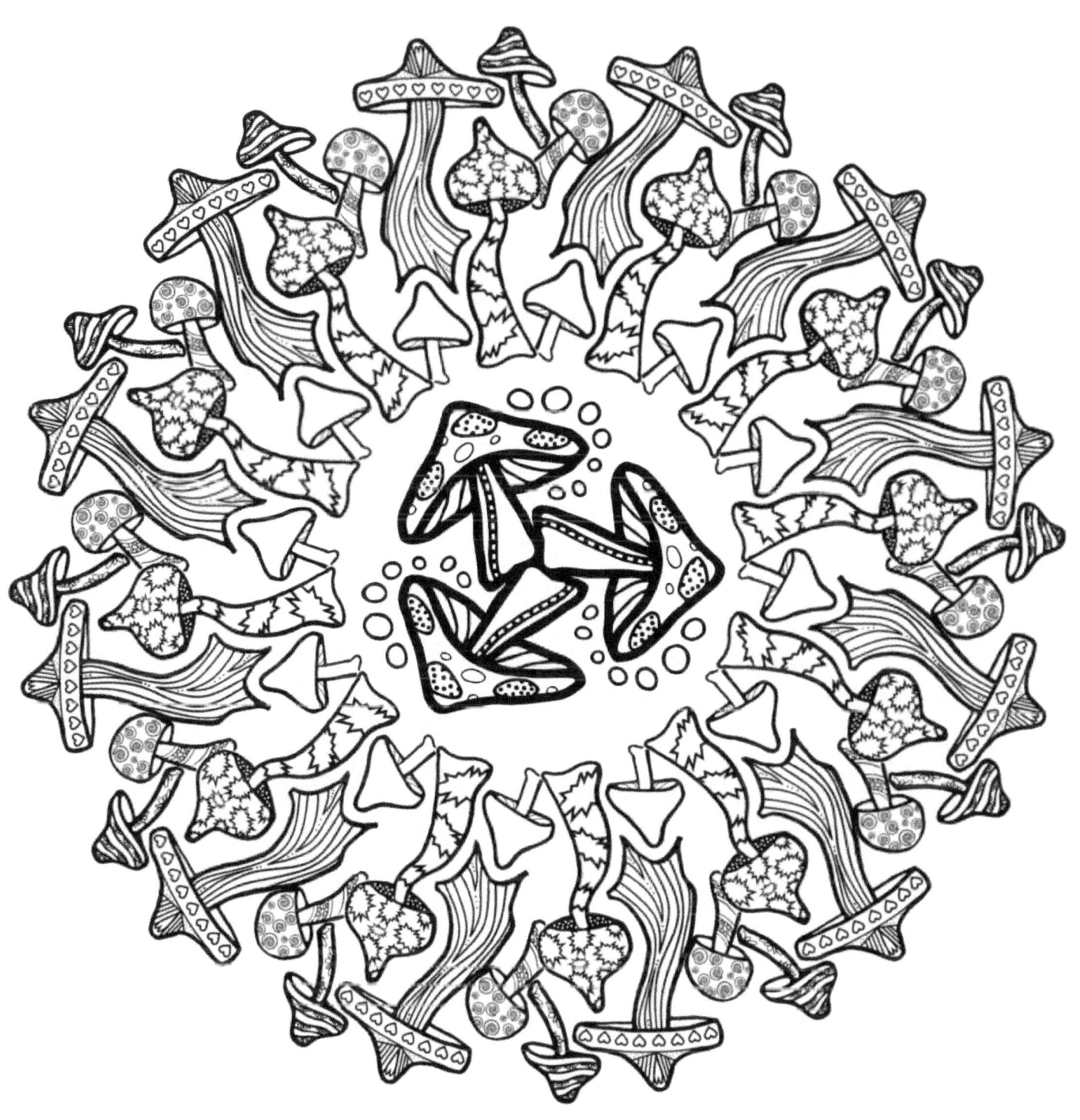

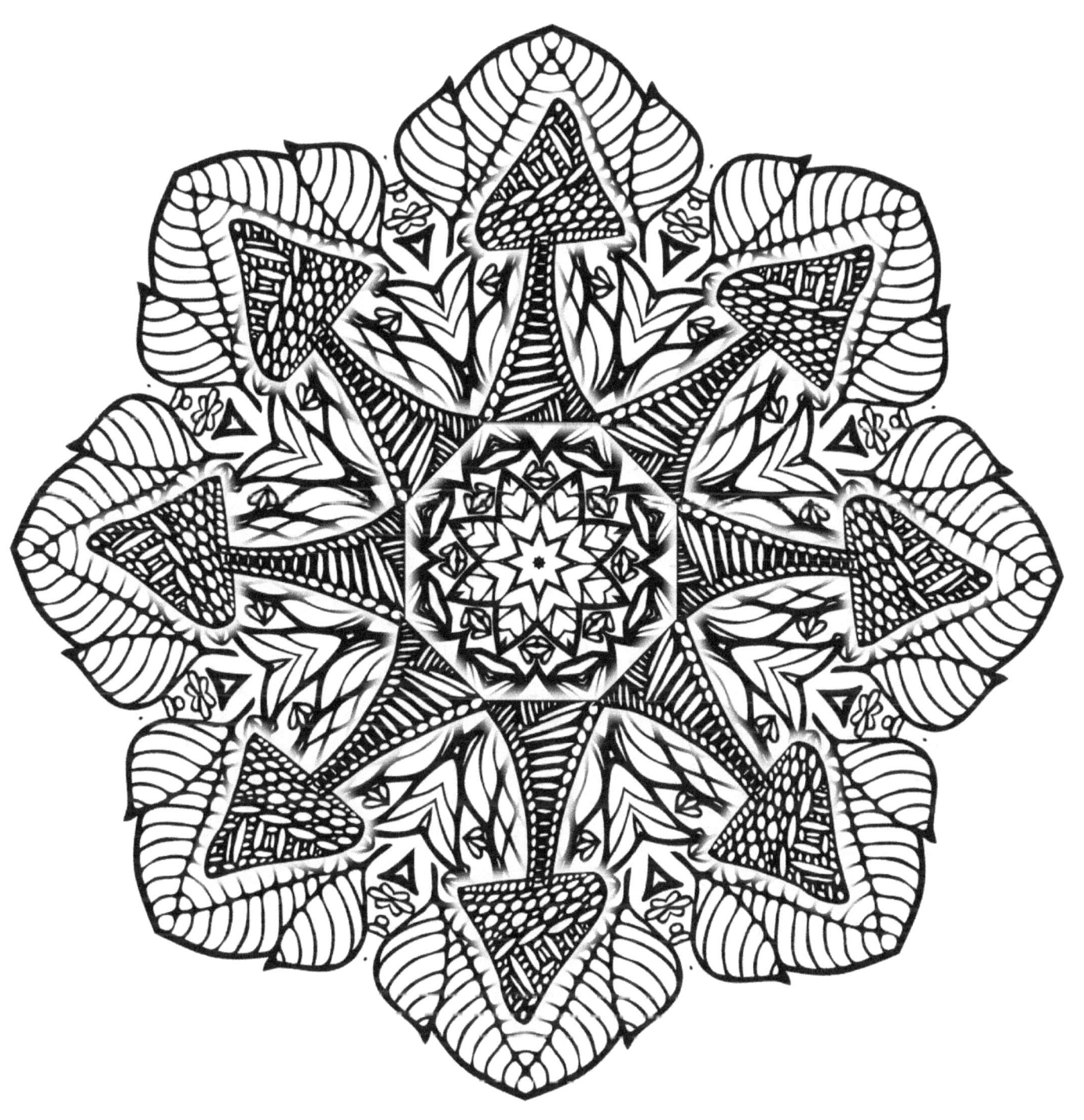

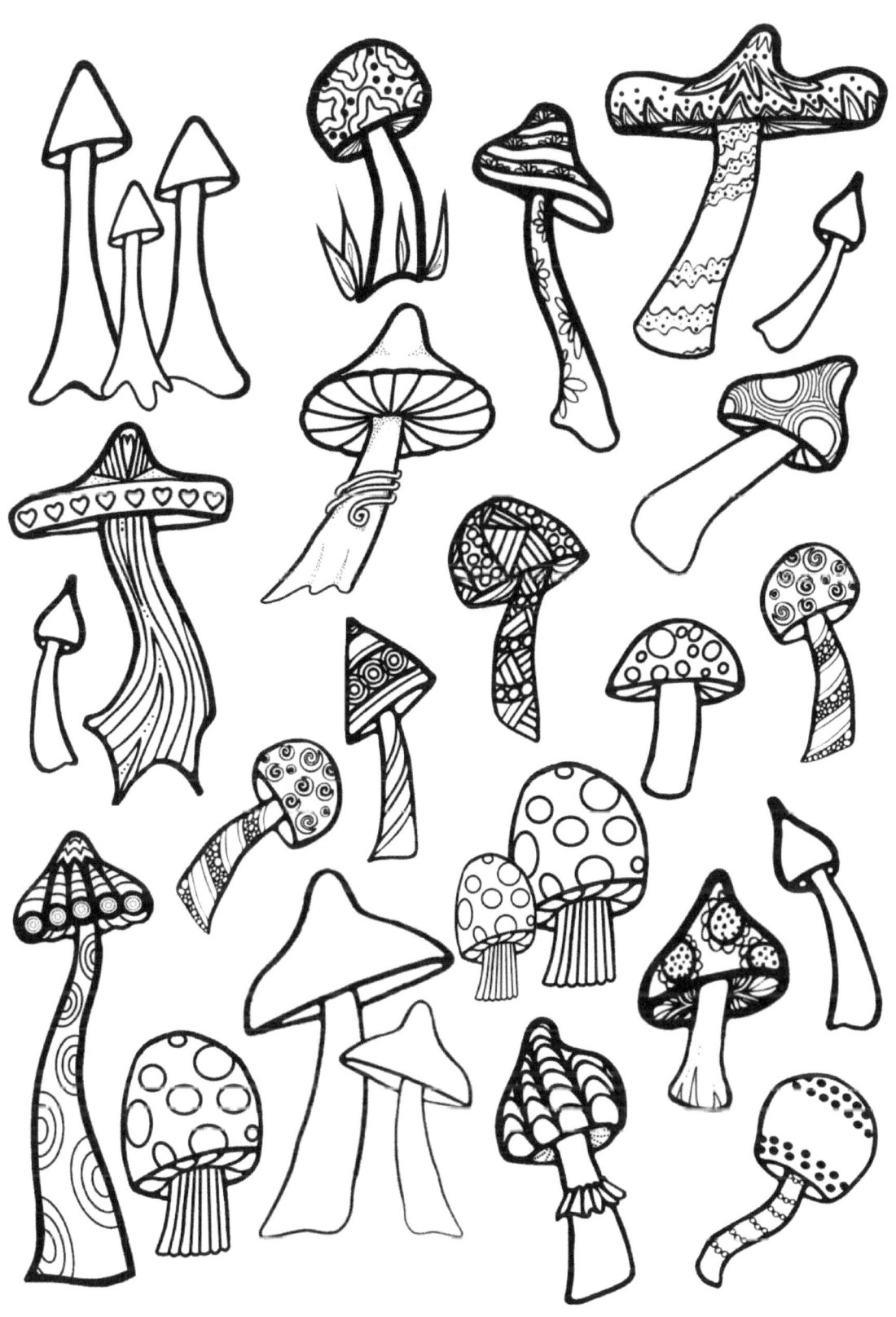

Like this book?

(♥ Thank you for purchasing it. ♥)
We'd Love for you to leave a review

Want more books like this one?

1. Follow me on *Facebook* @ **Magical Design Studios** - for regular *Free Downloads,* updates and announcements.
2. Join the Mailing List to get **5 free exclusive downloads immediately**, and news of upcoming releases. Just Click the Tab on our Facebook page & sign up, or go to **http://MagicalDesignStudios.com**
3. Follow my *Twitter* Feed. **@MagicalDsign**
4. Follow my author page on **Amazon**
5. Join us on the **Mushroom Magic Coloring Group** - https://www.facebook.com/groups/367995746886556/
6. Please leave a review on the site where you purchased the book.
7. Post your colorings (on my page or on your own). Tag me or **#MagicalDesignStudios** so we can see your images.

ABOUT THE AUTHOR KATIE DARDEN

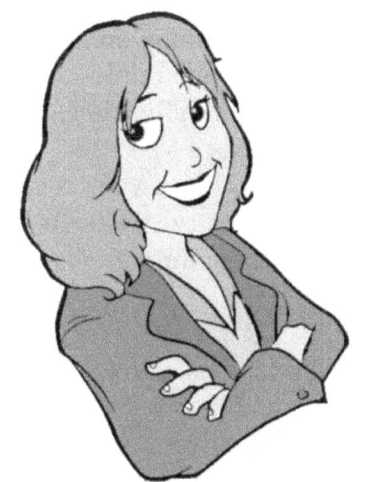

Katie Darden is an Amazon Bestselling Author of fiction and nonfiction books. She loves her strategic career and business books, but her fiction (and other fun stuff) is what's paying the bills.

In a not-too-distant past-life, she was a Business and Career Coach; Trainer; Speaker; and Internet Marketer with over 20 years experience in Human Resources, and Training & Development. Being an overachiever, she also built and managed several small businesses, enjoying all the benefits and challenges of being a serial entrepreneur.

She loves working with creative, innovative people, and small biz start-ups. For several years she focused on working with women entrepreneurs, winning awards for website design and managing local and national business networking groups with the National Association for Female Executives (NAFE). She is a 1997 graduate of Coach U, a founding member of Coachville and the Graduate School of Coaching, a certified Handwriting Expert, a registered and certified hypnotherapist, and Master Practitioner of Neuro Linguistic Programming (NLP). She's walked on 64 feet of burning coals with Tony Robbins in his Mastery University, and no longer has any fear of fire.

Currently she is focused on her writing. Among other things, she co-writes and co-illustrates children's books with her granddaughter Evalhena. Their first book is "The Sad Cloud Who Wanted to Make Friends". They have 3 more planned, but it's hard to focus if you are a young teenaged girl, LOL. Still, the proceeds of that book all go towards Evalhena's college education.

She's thrilled to finish this volume of fantasy mushrooms with her oldest grandson, Billy, and hopes they'll do another one soon. The proceeds of this book go towards defraying the costs of his education as he completes his degree in chemistry at a local college.

Being relatively right/left brain balanced, Katie is an artist in her "spare" time, designing and creating award-winning fused glass jewelry (more fire!) and painted fabric items for her Etsy stores - Fire Blessed Art and Magical Design. She considers herself fortunate to live on the far Northern Redwood Coast of California and to spend the rainiest 4 months every year in San Felipe, Mexico, on the Sea of Cortez.

Katie enjoys creating environments and opportunities for people to discover and express their natural gifts and talents. While several sources insist coloring is the next best thing to meditation, Katie, being an overachiever, finds designing coloring books even more relaxing than the actual coloring. She hopes you enjoy playing with your crayons and pens in her books.

ABOUT THE AUTHOR BILLY BUSH

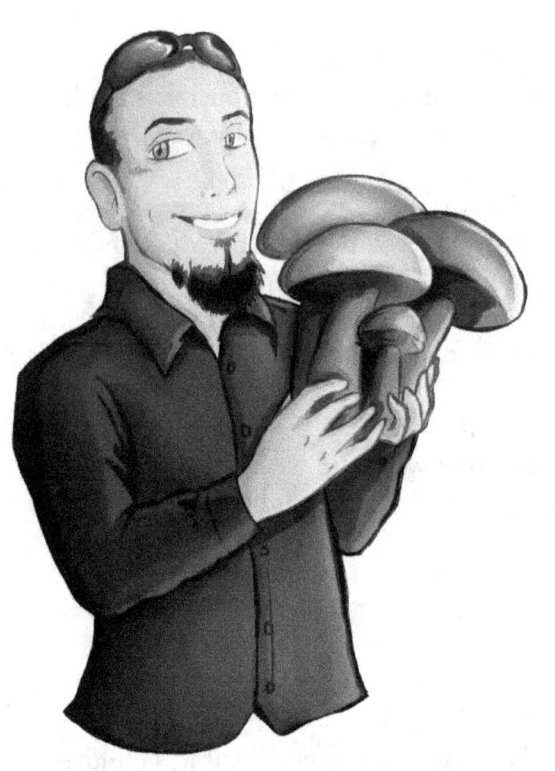

Billy Bush is an amateur mycologist, living on the edge of the great redwood rainforest, where multiple varieties of mushrooms propagate naturally. He is currently working really hard towards a Master's degree in Chemistry, and almost has his AA to show for it. In his spare time he likes to observe the beauty and diversity of life in the area, hiking through the forests and along the ocean.

With a strong mechanical ability and background, he takes after his father and both grandfathers, having a good understanding of spatial relationships and structural order. At one time he believed he wasn't creative, but has since learned to just let that energy flow through him. He's a musician as well as an artist, and likes to think of his drawings as a way to channel his music into a physical and visual form.

He loves learning new things about the world, and helping the people who come into his life. He hopes his art will inspire others to open up to their own creative expression.

Color Sample Chart
Use this chart to test your pencils, pens, etc. on this paper

Brand/Color	Sample	Brand/Color	Sample	Brand/Color	Sample